See Me Beautiful

Patricia Jamie Lee, MA

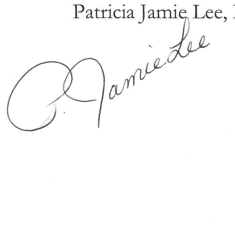

Many Kites Press

Rapid City, SD

Printed in the United States

Originally printed in 1987 as
Feeling Good About Feeling Bad
Revised and reprinted in 2011
by Many Kites Press

www.manykites.org

ISBN 978-0-9618469-6-1

Other Books
by Patricia Jamie Lee

Fiction

Washaka—The Bear Dreamer

Albert's Manuscript

One Drum

The Wind of a Thousand Years,
story booklet for The Bead People
International Peace Project
www.thebeadpeople.org

Nonfiction

The Lonely Place
Revisioning Adolescence and the Rite of Passage

The Genealogy of the Soul
A Personal Guide to Family Constellation Work

Table of Contents

Author's Note

It is an interesting task to re-enter a book I wrote over twenty years ago with the idea of adding a bit of spit and polish to it. *Feeling Good About Feeling Bad* was a labor of love for me back in the early days of my recovery and discovery programs. Although I had a computer back then, the task of printing a book in 1987 was still tough. When my meager supply of books ran out recently, I had to ask myself whether this was a book that was ready to retire or a book that still wanted to be in the world. Since you are reading this foreword to the new revision, you know my decision.

So much has transpired since I first scribbled these words into a notebook. My life has repeatedly taken unpredictable twists and turns. I found my true mate, I left behind NLP training as a career, spent ten years writing radio documentary on native issues with Milt (my mate), wrote several novels and had a spiritual experience that rocked my world. I'm now a grandmother, a novelist, was a college instructor and eventually bought ten acres of land in northern MN and built a straw bale house, yet, I am still the me you see represented in the pages to follow. Probably the most important thing I've learned in two decades is that life is not circular but a spiral. Like the swirling seashell, we continue to add whorls and colors into our original, authentic self.

Probably the biggest change in my view of the world since first writing this book is that my thinking has become simplified. Instead of all the relationship building between the conscious and unconscious mind, I think instead in terms of just growing ourselves up. So many of us are living our lives trapped in childlike thinking and being, and all of the techniques presented here will help you to grow up.

For the most part, I've decided to leave the original text of *Feeling Good* alone although I like to think I'm also a better writer these days. I only smoothed a few sentences, cut some clutter, dropped a lot of punctuation marks, and expanded the section on levels of development. I also knocked out a couple of rambling chapters at the end. Other than these few changes, the only other thing I did was add a few personal notes and exercises at the end of the each chapter when I felt the urge. The one other thing I considered changing are the references to popular (at the time) books but even that serves as a reminder of how fleeting is our time here, and so I leave them be.

However, I still like the book and have been continually amazed at where the original 2,000 copies have been. I've had letters from Germany, South America, and other parts of the world. I've had orders from bookstores in places I've never been.

Just this morning I was sitting and chanting an ancient yogic text when I had the sharp realization that some day I will die and all of my ideas with me. I probably will not be a voice any will remember, not famous or wealthy as I had hoped in my youth. There is little that belongs to me except my own state of mind. For me, however, this is wealth beyond measure. I want only to serve the world in which I find myself. Let me know how you are doing. Contact and website information are in the back of the book.

Sincerely,

Jamie Lee

Chapter One:
A Blueprint for Life

For years people have referred to the unconscious mind as a kind of mysterious guru who will perform magic, if bidden, by using the right magic word. This idea of the unconscious mind was part of a mounting frustration I had with affirmations, positive mental attitude, positive visualization, and . . . well, you get my drift.

It wasn't working. I wasn't getting what I needed to be happy. I felt like scrooge in *The Christmas Carol.* Positive mental attitude . . . bah humbug! I nearly growled every time somebody told me to "think positively."

Scott Peck began his book, *The Road Less Traveled,* with the words, "Life is difficult." I agreed with him. I also agreed that thoughts are things, and that I needed to meditate, eat better, sleep more, make my bed, be a cheerful person, and pursue the American Dream. In short, I agreed with all of it—and none of it. I felt like there were two of me—one on the inside who knew who she was and one on the outside doing things according to the rules.

In the midst of my struggle, a friend gave me a medallion which I carried in my purse for years. I would take the coppery coin out and fiddle with it, reading the words printed on it over and over: "To Thine Own Self Be True." I wondered what it meant and how in the world a person did it.

Finally, I saw that I was living my life according to other people's rules and somehow abandoning my own greatest desires. Instead of discovering the deeper side of my own nature, I was reaching for the quick fix. I'd sit before a lighted candle waiting for illumination with no earthly idea what it was I wanted to be illuminated about. I expected magic—and got little or nothing because I lacked a basic knowledge about the mind and how it works.

By the early eighties I was at the lowest point in my life. My marriage was ending, a melancholy depression hung about my head like a cloud, and I was angry. This is it, all of it? Life was a

1

battle and I was losing. Now I see that my growth process was like a pregnancy—I just got heavier and heavier until I could no longer ignore it and had to do something to get relief.

Relief came in the form of counseling, thirty days of treatment for co-dependency, and years of attending support groups and learning to reach out to others. That was what I now consider the *first stage* of my recovery—getting out of utter chaos and depression.

When I look around the world, I see many people reach this point and then stop—as if just getting out of chaos is enough. I believe there is so much more to be done once we reach this basic level of comfort and relief from chaos. In fact, this is where the fun begins, where personal growth becomes a true expansion of the self.

The tools presented in this book I used with myself first. When I began using them with clients, I saw them also begin to change and grow again. As I grew, my tool kit also grew until I could no longer present it all in a morning lecture. This book is a result of that overflow of ideas—about getting more and more from life.

Many of the tools are my own and others I've gleaned from keen minds and from the field of Neurolinguistic Programming. I try to give credit where credit is due.

The tools presented here are for the person in what I call Level Two and Level Three Recovery. If you are still living in Level One chaos, you'll not have the time, energy, or interest to go this far into your own psyche. Better to use your precious energy to get out of the chaos—quit drinking, get out of the abusive relationship and find a safe place. And then pick up this book and begin to explore its contents.

Chapter Two:
The Five Levels of Development

When we study psychology, we learn that children must go through certain phases of development in order to reach a healthy adulthood. As parents, we expect our little ones to have trouble regulating behavior and curiosity and to go through such things as the "terrible twos." Unfortunately, little attention has been given to the stages we grown children must go through to find our maturity. Life is an evolutionary process that occurs in stages very similar to the child's process. Here I use the word "Level" rather than stages to refer more to the internal process rather than the chronological stages of development.

Below is a summary of the levels of development described by Dabrowski in his *Theory of Positive Disin-tegration*. I first encountered this theory in a paper presented to the American Psychological Association in 1981 entitled, *Inner Conflict As A Path To Higher Development In Women* by Linda Silverman and Elizabeth Schuppin.

My friend, Deb, who suffers from multiple sclerosis, got this paper at a treatment center and gave me a copy. At that time, I was restless with recovery and was wondering about life *after* the twelve steps. The program seemed to work fine—as long as you were suffering, but when I wanted to reach for some new horizon, I felt lost and alone. As I read this paper, I had an explosive realization about where I was trying to get to. Only later, as I was tracking down the source of this paper, did I discover Dabrowski's theory.

I present the levels here in my own shorthand because they form the foundation of this book. To make the levels a bit clearer, I describe them first as an aspect of normal childhood development followed by how the same behaviors appear in a developing adult.

3

Level One: Chaos

Level One is chaos. Picture the infant grabbing out to the world and pulling it toward him like a tablecloth on a table. The infant or small child is literally "eating" his world without knowledge or understanding of what he eats. His immature brain is rapidly firing and stretching in the effort to bring in language, coordination, and an understanding of his relationship to the world and to others. All of this chaotic activity is expected and anticipated by the parent.

Adult chaos, however, is quite different. It may still be related to the erratic activities of the brain but the results are neither anticipated nor expected. Adults stuck in Level One are unable to manage their own brains effectively and show serious signs of chaos with irresponsible finances, obsessive eating or drinking, and abusive behavior or mental illness. The chaos can be noisy and dangerous and aimed outward at the world—or turned inward to become a whittling away of any sense of self. Examples of a person in Level One are the abusive alcoholic, the chronically depressed, the criminal or the adult unable to face the responsibility and reality of his or her life.

Level Two: The Rules

The movement from Level Two occurs when we adopt a set of rules which puts chaos to rest. In the small child, when the brain reaches a level of stability he is suddenly able to understand that if he follows a few simple rules, Mommy and Daddy will not get angry or upset. This level sees the child into and through elementary school. Those who have spent time with small children will realize that routines and schedules and rules give the child a sense of security. They actually become attached to the schedule if the parents present it.

Likewise, a set of rules can put chaos to rest for adults. In Level Two the chaotic adult suddenly adopts a system or set of rules and chaos abates. The change is often quick, a conversion of sorts. Some of the best examples of this are the chaotic alcoholic finding the 12-Steps of Alcoholics Anonymous or the individual who is saved or born again by a set of religious rules. The new structure allows his or her life to change for the better.

Level Two structures can be provided from many different directions such as religion, a new job, a strong relationship, a wellness program—even some multi-level marketing programs such as Amway can provide such structure.

Occasionally the vulnerable adult caught in chaos adopts a set of rules that is harmful. Consider gangs, cults and the Jim Jones or the David Koresh followers who lost their lives because they found and adopted a dangerous set of rules.

It became clear to me as I put these ideas into practice with clients, that one person, such as a therapist or spouse or even a parent, is not enough to provide adequate support and rules for stabilization. The individual in chaos needs the additional support of a social structure. Embracing this Level Two structure stabilizes us and allows us the time and energy we need to advance us toward further growth.

Level Three: Questioning the Rules

Level Three is one of the most fascinating levels of human development. Here, if (and only if) the individual has found security and safety in the earlier set of rules, he then moves on to Level three or questioning the rules. This is normal development. In families, it is called *adolescence*.

At this level, questioning the rules of the earlier struc-tures indicate that we are now beginning to self-define. Although it is a signal of growth, this rebellious period is what parents and teachers struggle with in the teen. We think we must crunch them back into the shape they had when they were good, rule-abiding children. This is like thinking we can stop a foot from growing if we buy a smaller size shoe.

This was the place I arrived when the recovery program began to feel more like limitation than enlightenment.

As I worked with these concepts, I began to recognize that each client was presenting problems from different levels of development. The woman who couldn't tolerate my urging her to seek a future vision would demand in a frustrated voice, "Yes, but what do I do?" She clearly wanted the structure and rules needed to put chaos to rest. On the other hand, clients who were firmly established in a social order gladly engaged the question, "What do you want? What is your vision of the future?"

It is important to note that this deep questioning of beliefs, wants, and desires can look very much like Level One chaos. It is a painful time of questioning the very foundation of our lives and searching for personal definition and meaning, a stretch toward the higher levels of development.

In Level Three, we have serious psychic growing pains and, although similar to chaos, it is not. We must be very careful here to choose teachers, therapists, and helpers who are just a little further down the road and not at an earlier level. In Level Three we are explorers of the cosmos, and travelers on the life path searching for what is possible.

Level Four: Self-Definition

This level is obtained only after many years of self-examination, inquiry, and deciding which rules apply at what time. The person in Level Four knows his or her deepest goals—and which rules to follow and which ones to break. She is able to sort and toss massive amounts of input and take only what is relevant to her. She knows how to express herself without anger, passive-aggressive behavior, or manipulation. We should all long for this level or the next for our children and ourselves.

Level Five: Self-Actualization

This highest level of development is only rarely obtained by those who have carefully traveled the previous paths. This person is now dedicated to a higher goal of service. It's as if this place exists far beyond the smaller human ego and its mundane hungers.

If you are fortunate enough to come in contact with one of these individuals, you will know it. He or she is completely self-contained, almost beyond personal desire, living at a high moral level and, most often, working for the greater good of mankind.

These levels are not clearly defined limits with boundaries and borders. Also, we can attain a new level but can be tossed back to an earlier level by tragedy or a new round of chaos. For example, the death of a loved one can cause chaos to re-emerge and send us scrambling for a Level Two support system. I use these levels here as a way to organize our thoughts. Knowing where we stand is the beginning of being able to shift direction.

I remember feeling guilty about beginning to question the rules within the recovery program. Didn't they save my life? Was I so ungrateful? Yet a small voice in the back of my mind was crying out, "But there has to be more. I still want more."

Just reaching a comfort zone, free from chaos, was not enough for me. The ache in my middle never goes away, and I don't expect it will until I'm gone from this place. It has become my best friend; it pushes and nudges me on, even when I think I've finally gotten *there*.

If you are asking yourself, "Is this it? Isn't there more?" then this book has come into your hands for the right reasons.

The following chapters move from the big picture to finer and finer pieces of inner awareness. The goal of the contents and the exercises is to encourage us to become our own teacher, guide or therapist and to build a temple based on who we are on the inside, not who we think we should be or could be. This journey begins by stressing the most important relationship we'll ever build—the one with our own self.

Read this book from beginning to end and take time to personalize it. The examples of client's stories have been scrambled and the names changed to protect the identities of specific individuals. Also, I'll mix up the he/she examples randomly to include both sexes.

Chapter Three
It's Just Common Sense

Understanding the Unconscious Mind

The unconscious mind is an ambiguous creature. We actually know very little about this mysterious part of the mind and yet mountains of literature have been written on the subject. People talk about the unconscious mind as if it were a good neighbor—but maybe one they don't know very well. Let's at least attempt our own definition.

The conscious mind refers to the waking brain, the state of mind that allows us to move through the day making moment by moment choices about what to eat for break-fast, what to wear that day, or what action to take next, etc.

On the other hand, the unconscious mind is often called *the deeper mind,* although I question the use of the word *deeper.* With all the mystery surrounding the unconscious mind it is easy to have the mistaken notion that the body has to be in a special state in order to gain information from the unconscious or that we have to be a yogi or a psychic in order to reach this part of our inner self.

Rollo May in *The Courage to Create,* said the unconscious mind can only go to work after we have studied a problem, fed in new information, and consciously sought an answer. In other words, without *conscious* input, the *unconscious* mind is in the dark.

There are many theories that the unconscious is the doorway to an even greater knowledge, a collective unconscious or an extrasensory awareness. We have all experienced those numinous moments when some elusive thought suddenly becomes crystal clear or synchronicity and spiritual alignment appear from nowhere but, for our purposes here, let's consider that exploring the greater capacity of the unconscious mind would be a graduate course and we are still freshmen. Let's keep it simple. Later we can refine and explore further.

The unconscious is not special. It must be fed infor-mation

in order to provide answers. For example, at one point I was confused about the best marketing approach to take for my seminar business and a positive mental attitude friend suggested I meditate and *go inside* and ask my unconscious for the right answers. The truth was, I lacked information and no amount of *going inside* would provide that if it had never been placed there. I needed to study marketing techniques.

Having said that, we can also acknowledge that we get unconscious information easier when we are in a slight trance such as on a long drive, waiting in a doctor's office, or just staring out of a window on a rainy day, but this is only because there is less daily chatter from the conscious mind.

On the level of physiology, we are actually talking about brain development and the neurological ability to make finer and finer connections via neural structures, dendrites, and all that jazz. The conscious mind runs the daily grind; the unconscious operates behind the scenes to assist us.

Why do we have an unconscious mind? What purpose does it serve? Have you ever really thought about thinking and the complex process that allows us to do an unusual activity like creating *thoughts*?

Thinking About Thinking

Thoughts are created by interactions between external and internal sensory information. The five senses (taste, smell, hearing, sight and touch) act as data collectors for the brain. They are constantly scanning the world and fun-neling in information and the brain then sorts and stores the information for later use. It would be impossible for us to *think clearly* if we had to hold all that information in conscious awareness. It would be like trying to catch a handful of confetti after throwing it into the air.

This is where the unconscious mind comes in. It has a greater capacity for storing information and is able to keep the conscious mind out of an overloaded state. It also acts as a messenger between the data bank (the brain) and conscious thought. Like sunglasses that filter out the sun's harmful rays, the unconscious protects the mind by acting as a filter that allows all information to be taken in—but only part of the information to reach the conscious mind.

For example, think about driving in heavy traffic. Even

10

External information, followed by internal sensations can recreate experiences that are not actually happening. This is called *thinking*. A thought can only be represented in the mind by a combination of these sensory experiences. Each thought is a complex sequence of internal words, images, feelings, tastes, and smells interacting with external material being picked up outside the body.

The ten senses, internal and external, are all we need to decipher the world and our place in it. At the simplest level, we need nothing else. Our goal here is to discover the many ways we create patterns of behavior, belief, and action. In order to do this we need to become detectives of our own process.

It would be wonderful if we had all been taught to heed the senses and pay careful attention to sensory data flowing in and around us. However, the reality is that much of it flows by unnoticed. We have learned to distrust the conscious and the unconscious mind and the sensory information they contain. Our process of thinking has been flawed by this distrust.

A Case for Common Sense

It is simple to understand the need to pay careful attention to the external sensory information. For example, we would not last long on the Los Angeles Freeway if we did not pay attention to the world around us. External senses guide us in the external world.

Early humans depended entirely on their senses to keep from being attacked by animals, eating bad food, or freezing to death in the winter. They also depended greatly on the intuitive, inner awareness of dreams and spiritual experience. Although our race has evolved and changed along with the world we live in, we still must rely on this external and internal information.

Have you ever noticed how often the word "sense" appears in daily language? When someone makes a foolish error, we say he lacks *common sense*. If an idea is flawed, we say it is *nonsense*. An extremely perceptive person has *extrasensory* awareness or is *sensitive*, and a great experience is *sensational*. It just makes *good sense* to learn more and more about the senses and the information they contain. They are the building blocks for effective living.

Books, workshops, and CDs are terrific sources of new information (food for thought) but worthless unless you take

13

the time to analyze and experience your own conscious and unconscious mind and the ten senses which hold the key to decoding the information held there.

Mapping out experiences and thought patterns does not have to be expensive or complicated once you know how to turn the attention inward. Everything you need—the ten senses and your own brain—are immediately available for use. The only other tool I suggest is this book, a pen and pad, and a quiet moment to be with your self in the neutral shelter outlined below.

Note: I can't resist cutting in again and adding a bit. Since the first edition of this book, I've met hundreds of people who spend their valuable resources running from teacher to teacher or workshop to workshop without ever slowing down enough to integrate and make the information practical. Without the tools to integrate and engage the material, these valuable resources are wasted. Please take time to learn how your brain works and integrate the material you are throwing at it.

Give Me Shelter

How often have you caught yourself doing something that doesn't fit who you want to be or feel that you are? I remember sniveling with a friend about a problem I was having when it suddenly dawned on me that she (the sniveler) was not the person I wanted to be.

How often do we engage in behaviors and thought forms that no longer seem right for us? Some people call the beliefs and rules feeding those negative behavior patterns *old tapes*. Like the woman in the following story, these old tapes often lose meaning in our current life.

Joan always cut the ends off her Christmas ham before she cooked it. At last, her husband asked her why she always cut the ends off. "Because my mother always did," was her reply. The next time they were at her mother's they asked Mom why she always cut the ends off of her ham before she cooked it. Mother replied, "Because your grandmother always did." Finally one Christmas they visited grandmother and asked her why she always cut the ends of the ham off before she cooked them. Grandmother said, "Because I never had a large enough roasting pan to cook the whole ham."

Beliefs and rituals are like that.

They are done automatically, without full realization of why it must be done just so. Many old beliefs originally kept the chaos of life under control, but they have a tendency to outlast the chaos, remaining in place long after the need for them has passed. They become habit, like the child that clings to the tattered blanket long after the need for extra security has diminished. After a point, it is just habit.

Rene Descartes', a seventeenth century philosopher, decided at an early age that the rules he was given as a child about how to live no longer fit for him. He decided to design his own set of rules, selecting only the beliefs, behaviors and lifestyle he wanted and discarding what seemed useless or weak.

However, before he began selecting what to keep and what to discard, he realized that a wise builder would never tear down an existing structure in order to rebuild without providing a temporary shelter, a place to stay in while the new construction was in progress. In order to secure this temporary shelter, Descartes' first selected a "middle of the road belief" that would protect him while he reconstructed his life.

Like Descartes', in order to reconstruct the existing structure of our lives, we must first go to a temporary shelter of neutral beliefs and rituals. Think of it like moving from one house to a temporary place while the new one is being built.

Pretend we have moved into a plain, brown-wrapper type of building. It has no terrific assets or aspirations, yet it has no major liabilities or structural flaws. It is not a slum—and not a castle—just a very generic sort of building that doesn't even know what its true function or purpose is. This is a temporary shelter, the place where all of our current beliefs and rules hang momentarily suspended while we have the opportunity to inspect each one carefully, deciding which to keep and which to discard. Our lives are crowded with rules about marriage, parenting, religion, God, selfishness, personal power, anger, and . . . well, there are plenty of rules.

Remember, just for now, we'll keep the temporary shelter free of the properties of any institutions, schools, churches, or other belief systems. Most of us have a strong tendency to use institutions to define the self—I am a mother, a Christian, a lawyer, a husband. We pick up the beliefs of the institutions to which we belong even though they may not fit.

Good. Are we firmly planted in our plain brown-wrapper building? To the drawing board then.

Exercises

How do we determine what beliefs and behaviors have been personally chosen and which have simply been programmed into our minds and become useless patterns? How do we tell if we are just following the *rules* or have begun to self-determine the rules? We all have embedded rules and beliefs about life and how to respond to circumstances. Start a notebook for examining your beliefs. Buy a cheap little wire-bound thing so nothing seems too important. Buying expensive journals makes us feel as if we need to say something *special*.

Now use the prompts below and write in a stream of consciousness manner to uncover hidden beliefs, key experiences, and life patterns. Remember, you don't have to be a writer to move a pen across a page. Pick one and just write. Let your unconscious mind direct your pen.

You don't need to do all of these prompts at once. Just choose one that resonates with you and, when you have finished, step back and look at what it says. What beliefs are embedded within the words? What drives your life? What do these words say about your political beliefs, your social idea of the world, the relationships you value or don't value? What old programming is revealed in those words?

1. What I remember most about the first grade is _____.

2. What I most don't want to remember about first grade is _____.

3. What I remember most about my parents' relationship is _____.

4. What I don't want to remember about my parents' relationship is _____.

5. When I feel backed into a corner I _____.

16

6. To me happily-ever-after is _____.

7. The person I like least in the world is _____
because _____.

8. The person I like most in the world
is_____ because _____.

9. The quality I most admire in others is
_____.

10. When I get angry, I am supposed to _____.

11. When I take real time for myself I feel like
_____.

12. The most powerful force in the universe is
_____.

13. The most destructive force in the universe is
_____.

14. When I am alone I like to _____.

15. When someone asks me to do something I don't
want to do, I feel _____.

Chapter Four
Dispelling Old Myths and Lies

You've now taken refuge in a temporary shelter and done a first preliminary examination of beliefs and patterns. What did you discover about the rules and old tapes that drive your life? What are they? Where did they come from? Do they add to life—or take away from it?

Old rules are often half-truths fed to us by our culture. I once asked a talented and artistic client, "What is the most selfish thing you can imagine doing?"

Without a second thought she said, "Let go of all the time consuming junk and pursue my art full time."

In what way is this selfish? For her, using a God-given gift equals selfishness. This is an old belief that needs to be cleared. Once, during a workshop, I asked participants to introduce themselves by describing "the most outrageous thing you could imagine doing." Oddly, as we went around the circle, the *outrageous* ideas did not seem out there at all but curiously close to the heart.

The struggle between a belief system and what our heart truly desires is often the source of emotional pain. We want what we want but somehow feel like doing that would be wrong. Outdated beliefs vs. inner desires keep us pulling in opposing directions like children in an endless tug-o-war. To end the struggle, one side must let go of the rope. We have to stop doing what no longer fits.

A question often asked by clients when I push them to reach higher is, "But am I just being selfish?" Becoming all that you can be is not selfish—everybody benefits. Giving half of your self to a cause or project—when the heart is not really in it—is selfish. Besides, maybe if we quit participating in clubs or institutions that no longer fit us, they would just die a natural death, and we would all be happier for it.

As children we depended upon parents or other adults to give us the rules by which to live. Unfortunately, too many rules were for their convenience rather than for our benefit. We were taught to set aside our needs and passions. Rules that taught us to ignore the unconscious mind and the inner self became myths or lies and not current reality. We will carefully inspect a few of the most common myths here.

Note: The above tug and pull was best defined for me in later years by the work of Robert Fritz in *The Path of Least Resistance*. He says that a tension system set up between two opposing beliefs creates an oscillating structure which traps us in a limiting movement between the two. He calls this "structural conflict." This opposing structure cannot be resolved except by creating a brand new tension system between current reality and what it is our heart desires.

The time I spent studying with Robert and his wife, Rosalind, have been one of the biggest contributions to how I do my life since NLP. I learned that all attempts to resolve these opposing structures are a waste of time. He says old beliefs create deeply embedded "hidden opinions" of our selves. For example, if I have a hidden opinion of myself that I am not good enough or smart enough, no amount of study, gaining degrees, etc. will alleviate that opinion. Instead, I now do as Rosalind recommended to me and simply shake hands with that opinion and then move toward creating what I want. We simply push on and build an entirely new structure based on what we want.

The First Lie–Don't Be Who You Are

The first lie and the hardest lie came with the message from the adults, "Don't be who you are." This rule becomes an insidious double bind both for children and adults. How can I *not* be who I am?

The message came at a critical time when we were first beginning to define and understand who we were. When we daydreamed they said pay attention; when we created with crayons, they said stay in the lines; when we wanted to dance and play, we sat in hard little desks in a row; and when we wanted to sing, the message was *hush*.

We learned that it was more important to be what they wanted us to be than to be what we were. Children are born with little capacity for surviving alone. We need adult approval and love. In fact, when there is a danger of the love being

20

withdrawn, a child often willingly sets aside exploration of self or saves it for private times when he can be who he is—without the adults watching.

The woman artist I mentioned above could remember being totally awed by her first box of crayons at age two and a half. How was she made to feel selfish about this gift?

Guilt becomes a normal way of life when it is not alright to be who we are. If we grew up with this rule, we fear that if the adults catch us being who we are, they will surely find us unlovable—and it is terrifying to feel unloved. A child who is not loved suffers and sometimes dies, as if food or shelter were being withheld. He cannot risk losing that love and learns quickly to play by the adult's rules.

So, we learned to pretend—to be happy when we are sad, nice when we feel ornery, satisfied when we are discontented. In fact, we learned to lie first to others—and then to ourselves. We did not learn to respond to the self.

The Second Lie—If You Can't See It, It Doesn't Exist

Descartes' greatest contribution to society was the development of the *scientific method*—a method for systematically studying the natural world. Basically, he proposed that if we can't see it or prove it by measurable means it does not exist. This simple method has advanced our knowledge of the physical world beyond expectation. However, the scientific method has also discouraged us from further exploration of our own inner reality because it is subjective and cannot easily be proven and validated. As a result, we learned to pay more attention to the external world and less to the internal world.

Now here is the paradox. Read carefully. The scientific method resulted from an interpretation Descartes' made of *three of his own dreams*. The scientific method is based on dream information—totally opposite from what science promotes as a real measure of the natural world.

In studying the history of great writers, artists, scientists, and philosophers we find a common thread of greatness—they trusted their internal, unconscious responses even though internal reality could not be proven or validated in any way. Thomas Edison, Eli Whitney, Einstein, Galileo, Newton, and

21

Da Vinci—all went about proving their ideas after the first intuitive flash.

What if these incredible people had accepted the *rule* that they should ignore subjective reality and depend only on what is observable or measurable? What if they had ignored the inner reality that lent so much to their great contributions? What if Descartes' had recalled the three dreams—and then passed them off as *silly*?

Emerson, in his *Essay on Self-Reliance*, says "In every work of genius we see our own rejected thoughts." Descartes' could have rejected his dreams and the methods for understanding and testing the natural world would have gone undeveloped.

There are far too many dream-dashers in the modern world—too many rules about being realistic, about what it is possible to accomplish, and how to measure personal value with dollar signs. The realism of dreams and dollar signs is that you have to dream and believe in your dreams, and pursue your dreams in order to make dollars on dreams.

Henry Ford did not let dollar signs influence his dream. He just put himself in perpetual motion and made it happen without stopping to wonder what *they* would think. He just had a dream—and belief in a dream—and perpetual motion. That is the stuff of dreams.

I could cite case after case of rags-to-riches founded on the strength of a dream or single vision. In his book, *Thinking About Thinking With NLP*, Joseph Yeager said, "Goals come from dreams—or better yet, goals are dreams. Dreamers in history have been alternately vilified and glorified depending on the outcome of their dreams."

If only we trusted our dreams—our heart's desires. Yeager also said, "A goal may be what you settle for when what you really want seems unattainable."

Dreams and intuitive impulse come from the deeper side of us, from the unconscious mind that stores the information and knows what the spark, the desire, the dream is really about. The unconscious knows what is possible for us to accomplish, what we are worth, and what needs to happen to make it real. It wouldn't provide a dream that wasn't possible to achieve.

Note: This discussion seems a bit at odds from what I said earlier about how information must be first placed in the unconscious in order for it to resurface later as knowledge. Perhaps the confusion can be resolved by suggesting that there is something beyond the unconscious, a super-conscious mind where resides the person we are meant to be. I don't want to divert into a spiritual discussion, yet the richest part of my development since first writing this book relates to impulse, intuition, and a knowing self that guides the process or is tuned into a finer impulse. I'll just let this sit here as a footnote.

The Third Lie—But I Am Only One Person. What Can I Do?

Apathy. Learned helplessness. Insignificance. I can't make a difference in the world . . . it is so large and I am so small. This lie has a serious effect on how we act. This is the first and second lie taking their toll on us. This attitude says "I don't count," and points to low self worth and no personal power. If we ever totally accept and believe that life is meaningless, we have lost the ability to choose the direction of our own life.

Accept the learned helplessness and there is no meaning or purpose in life. People who come too close to believing this often respond in one of two ways—they aggressively and greedily seek power and control or they give away all power and control and become blind followers or victims.

A classic example of this is an abusive marital relationship. Jack feels helpless so he takes control of the feeling by becoming violent with his wife Jane. Jane feels helpless and allows her self to be victimized for years thinking she has no other choice. In feeling helpless, they both *become* helpless and unable to change, but the real problem is the loss of choice for each of them.

Of course, one person alone does not have the power to control the events of the world. Yet one plus one plus one at work changing the events of the inner world can transform a universe.

We really only have one requirement, one job in life, and that is to become all that it is possible for us to become. At birth, from whatever source, we are given a few precious hot coals, little sparks that begin to light the direction of our lives. Maybe we love to entertain, love nature, love to sing or write or draw or we love the challenge of following a problem through from beginning to end. These sparks heat us up and make us feel fully alive.

To become all that is possible we need to add fuel and then fan those coals into high intensity flames that offer light and consolation to the world. This is the way to change the world. This is the way for just one person to make a difference.

You may be unsure what the hot coal or the spark is for you, but stay with it and fill in the blanks as you go. Remember that the first phase is just inspecting the initial structure of rules and beliefs. Reconstruction comes later.

Another little trap we can fall into is spending countless hours trying to determine if there is a fancy, huge design already laid out for us like a script sitting on someone's desk with our name on it. This is illusion, a stream we get caught in that sweeps us off the trail. If we spend enormous time and energy trying to find the greater design, we miss the present moment. The conscious mind's primary job is to do whatever is placed in front of it by the unconscious and to continue feeding information into that unconscious store-house of knowledge.

However, when inner and outer self come into alignment, we may begin to notice unusual coincidences and actions that seem to slide right into place as if we had nothing to do with them.

The Fourth Lie—Responsibility Equals Slavery

The word *responsibility* can be so ominous. For years I thought my main goal in life was to learn to be responsible, and that responsibility meant maturity and adulthood in our society. I had never really thought about the world *responsibility* and what it meant to me. Have you ever defined it for yourself? Try this.

Say the word *responsibility* to yourself. What does it conjure up? Is it a positive or a negative thought? Does it make you squirm a bit? Are you thinking of a lifetime of doing things you don't want to do? Is that thought a little uncomfortable?

Now, split the word into two words by saying it very slowly;

> . . . response-ibility
> . . . response-ability
> . . . the ability to respond

The word takes on a different meaning when you do that,

24

doesn't it?

Responsibility does not mean slavery to a clock, a job, a family or the almighty dollar. It means *the ability to respond.* Imagine being nursed by a society that praised individual responsiveness and self-awareness? If the partnership between the conscious self and unconscious self were nurtured and tended from the beginning, we would perhaps not struggle so in this human life.

In some remote cultures the people are still required to respond to unconscious awareness. For example, in one culture, if a person has a dream about another person in the village, he is *required* to go to that person and explain the details of the dream to the other person. The unconscious dream-self is treated respectfully, almost reverently. This respect and careful attention to the unconscious is what counts—attention to the images, sounds, words, and feelings from the inner world. We still make the conscious decisions about how to act on what is given—that is the *ability* part of response-ability. With practice and experience, the conscious and unconscious mind can become a powerful team.

In my experiences helping people grow and change, I've noticed that many problems erupt from being unwilling or unable to respond to the first gut feeling. Refusal to act on first responses leads to resentment, overload, or putting up with unacceptable or inappropriate behavior from a mate, child, or boss. The results of this refusal to respond are far more destructive than acting on the gut feeling. Like taking a true/false test, your first response is usually the best. However, this does not mean going with your first knee-jerk response to things but to have the ability to examine and choose the right response.

For example, Marge was married to a man who fancied himself a comedian and would continuously poke fun at any of her comments or questions. Every time he did this, Marge felt sick, but she told herself that she was just being *too sensitive.* She suffered from chronic depression—but in the nine years of living with this verbal abuse, she had never once asked him to stop doing it.

Failure to pay attention to small unconscious signals can result in big problems. Often we become so numb to any sensations that we cannot even pinpoint the triggers to which

25

we are actually responding. Marge feared there was something seriously wrong because her depression had taken on such large proportions.

Even sitting in dull, endless meetings and forcing yourself to stay there or serving on meaningless committees because you *should* take a toll on your responsiveness. Many problems come from judging the initial response or gut feeling and acting on our *judgment* of it rather than on the true response. This is the next faulty stone in our foundation.

The Fifth Lie—There Are Good and Bad Feelings

We have been taught there is such a thing as good feelings and bad feelings. In truth, feelings cannot be good or bad—feelings just are. They are the messengers between the conscious and unconscious mind, a way of transmitting information from one to the other. To call some feelings good and others bad is a flaw in our thinking. This was why I disliked the message of the positive mental attitude folks—they suggest that there are certain feelings I should work towards eliminating if I want to be a happy person.

The word *feeling* tends to be kind of a catch-all word; it means emotions, responses, physical sensations, and some thoughts. It is this catch-all phenomenon which adds to the confusion about what is happening inside our own brains.

For our purposes here, a feeling is simply a response to a stimulus—a reaction to what is happening around us or inside of our own heads. Like a fever, feelings come to let us know something is going. Whatever name we give the feelings, they are always a response in the body. We attach many names to them as a way to sort our reality. As we progress, we will make finer and finer distinctions about these responses.

Words are meant to define our reality. For example, various cultures have different ways to define *snow*. A person in Peru needs only one word to define snow. A skier needs several words that define the different snow conditions for skiing. An Eskimo in Alaska has thirty-one words to define snow. As our need to understand ourselves grows, so does our need to make finer distinctions between the various feelings and inner responses.

To truly know the self, we must let go of our need to act as judge and jury of feelings and gut responses. Naturally, some responses are more pleasant or less pleasant, but they are never good or bad. It is dangerous to miss the unconscious messages and refuse to respond.

Think about it. I become aware of a certain bodily response (a tight gut, a blush, damp palms) and, as soon as I notice the first sensation, I give it a name (anxious?) and often develop a new set of responses about the initial feeling. Here is where life gets complicated. Once I've named the sensation and attached a feeling, I'm already moving away from the primary response and forming a secondary response about it.

The key word here is *about*. If we are having feelings *about* feelings—especially feelings that imply judgment or dislike, feelings we'd rather dump or discard—then we are missing vital information needed to adjust the pattern or belief that the primary sensation is revealing. And often the secondary set of responses or how we feel *about* the feeling is usually more uncomfortable than the original feeling.

If this is true, then we may begin to explain, rationalize, and otherwise abuse the precious gift of our initial, primary response and the lessons it contains. If you imagine a stone plopping into water, it sinks in one spot but the water begins to ripple out until it is far removed from where the stone first hit the water.

If we accept the idea that there are no good or bad feelings, just sensations meant to guide us toward making better choices, all first feelings (even the uncomfortable ones) become an ebb and flow pattern that encourage personal growth.

Here is an example. Say you have a co-worker who, for whatever reason, doesn't like you. He never says a word, but begins to sabotage you in ways that make your work appear shabby and sublevel to your ability. You like your work and the co-worker until it becomes obvious what he is doing.

At first you roll with the punches, and then you begin to justify *his* behavior (I must be imagining . . .) but an element of dis-ease is introduced. This uneasiness increases as you discover another and another of these stunts until at last your dis-ease is intense enough that you must act to relieve the pressure of your feelings. You are uncomfortable and in conflict.

Old beliefs and patterns may convince you to ignore your initial feeling and muster on. However, this situation does not call for *thinking about the feeling* or trying to figure out why this person is doing this or inspecting all of your activities and motives and wondering what will happen next. Thinking *about* the feeling can only lead to potential disaster—the loss of a job or an angry falling-out with the co-worker.

We need to examine our feelings and act. We cannot simply ignore the feeling or stuff it down and beat ourselves up for being too sensitive or for imagining things.

Ignoring an inner signal forces the primary feeling to build until the response potential reaches the point of exploding. Some people call this stuffing your emotions. If allowed to build to this level, there is a danger of acting in ways that are not appropriate. Either that or you implode and turn the feelings back in on yourself by judging them harshly, thus judging yourself harshly.

Depression is often the result of doing this. I've often heard that depression is "anger turned inward."

Do you recall the last time you blew up at someone over some small thing? That person was treating you in some unacceptable way, and you had a strong response, but instead of acting according to the earliest response, you talked yourself out of it by saying, "I shouldn't feel this way—look at all he has done for me." You stuffed your feelings down until one day you blew your top. Then you berated yourself again by cursing and saying harshly, "I have got to learn to control my emotions better."

Here is a great paradox in emotional control—the best way to control your emotions is to have less control and to respond earlier—at the first sign of discomfort.

There are no bad feelings. They serve a vital function similar to physical pain in indicating disease or disorder in the physical body. Emotional pain or discomfort is the signal light for knowing something is not working in our psyche. Actions can be deemed right or wrong—but feelings just are.

Well, you are in the plain wrapper building and have just done a first assessment of the state of your personal space. Is it constructed the way you want it? How have you treated the signals given by your unconscious? How many rules do you have that are not your own?

We have not even scratched the surface of the hundreds of belief systems and rules by which we operate our lives, but this is a beginning. In order to create a structure that has beauty and stability, we must first strengthen the foundation by fine-tuning our understanding of feelings and how we respond to them. Like the Eskimos and their thirty-one types of snow, success depends on how well we can distinguish the various feelings.

In rebuilding our house of the self, it is important to have a strong foundation and to discard what is weak. The myths and lies given to us early in life were faulty and now we are ready to put in their replacements.

Remember that your structure also has many nice features and qualities—you can keep what you like. Nothing is lost in this reconstruction phase—only added to.

Here I will ask you to make a preliminary leap in faith, to trust the foundation stones that I will lay out from the beginning. Some may fit for you and some may not, but this is a starting point, the beginning of the move from the plain-wrapper building to a structure of your own design.

Exercise:

Take your notebook and identify three or four instances when you "lost it" with another person or in a situation. Experiment with stepping back from the incident and then attempting to identify the first signals you received, the indicator that things were not going well.

This will feel a bit like running a movie backwards frame by frame. It is useful to deconstruct past moments to discover important "choice points" where another action could have been chosen.

When you identify them, write an alternative scenario in which you imagine yourself going to that person, staying adult, and dealing with the situation. Mental practice in-creases the probability that you will respond differently the next time.

Chapter Five
Building From the Ground Up

The First Foundation Stone:
Change is the only constant in life

Life is like a kaleidoscope. The patterns continually shift and change, and if the movement stops, life ceases to be interesting. The colors and shapes of the kaleidoscope are your past, present, and future blending and changing. There is no single pattern or place that we arrive at that is thee place. The richness of the moment depends upon the blend of where we came from—and where we are heading. Change is the only thing we can depend upon as a constant in life.

Whenever we take an existing composition and add ingredients—we have a new composition. If I take plain white flour and add yeast and water—I get bread. Self-awareness is like that. Just when I think I know myself, I change. I can never completely know myself as long as new information is being channeled in on the senses. New information equals new composition.

Even locked in a sensory deprivation chamber with no external sight or sound, the inner senses would begin to add data in the form of hallucinations and delusions. Whether it is the inner or outer senses adding information, the composition continually changes.

Change is the only constant, the only thing we can depend upon. When we have accepted change as a constant, then that is the one thing that won't change.

Look around. How many people do you know who have sold their souls for an illusion called security? It is the American Dream—work hard, get an education, get married, buy a house, buy a car, buy an IRA and you have arrived.

In reality, to refuse to risk and stretch into new territory is to risk losing it all. If we want more security—we have to risk more. One man I met thought that when he got an electrical engineering degree he would have made It.

The Second Foundation Stone:
We can never be always at anything

What words do you use to define yourself? I often ask my groups to take out a sheet of paper and write five words that they use to identify themselves. The lists usually cover the full range from foul adjectives to more common identifications like engineer or teacher or mother. Which five words would you use?

Take a minute and write them into your notebook.

1. _____
2. _____
3. _____
4. _____
5. _____

In order for the foundation of our new life structure to be stable and well-built, we have to probe the words we use to define ourselves. This includes both the external, socially-accepted words like teacher or husband and internal definitions like lazy, procrastinator, deadbeat, etc. The labels we attach to ourselves can often begin to define us rather than describe us.

There are the phrases that I call non-sense words that are popular today but do even less to help us define ourselves. Words like compassionate, self-worth, self-confident, Christian, etc, fit into this category.

The language we use to describe and define our lives plays an important and powerful role in determining what will happen next. It pays to listen to how we self-define. Be careful whenever the words "I am . . . " begin to fall off your tongue. We often use words to confine and restrict ourselves. Consider, for example, the limiting worlds these words can create:

I am . . .

     . . . a procrastinator,
     . . . not creative,
     . . . a loner,
     . . . not very smart,
     . . . learning disabled,
     . . . unhappy,
     . . . disorganized,

. . . lazy,
. . . depressed.

Every one of these self-definitions can lock us into a specific course of action defined by whatever history is attached to it. Not finishing one project does not make you a *procrastinator* forever. Not liking one part of a job does not make you *unhappy at work*. One down day does not make you *depressed*. Even a repeating pattern does not mean you are locked into that way of being for the rest of your life. Human beings are capable of evolving over time and replacing one pattern with something much more creative and generative.

What would happen if you concentrated only on the words I AM? Nothing more, nothing less, just I AM.

Using specific language is essential to growth and choosing our self-defining words and phrases can lead to positive change. Later, we will spend an entire chapter exploring the language, but the important thing for now is to begin listening to the words rolling out of our mouths, or in our minds, as well as listening to the language patterns in those close to us. We can train our ears to hear these restrictive patterns and change them.

Language reflects what the brain is doing. I remember being stuck in an *if only* pattern—if only I hadn't married, had children, quit grad school, stayed in South Dakota. I had a million *if onlies*. At last a good friend smiled and said wisely, "If only is lonely."

A final cautionary note here—we mustn't let others define us either. We must be especially careful of doctors or therapists who need to pin labels and diagnoses on clients for the purposes of billing out services. Life is full of loss and struggle and an almost painful reaching for new heights. To have ordinary life experience diagnosed as "illness" is a dangerous game. Suddenly we diagnosed as bi-polar or ADHD or depressed. Contrary to common thought, the mental health field is still in its infancy. Unfortunately, diagnostic trends are often driven by the drug companies instead of solid, physiological research. A drug will not help you to self-define and self evolve. In fact, it will sometimes deaden all of your natural signals and indicators sometimes making it even more

33

difficult to self-assess.

Part of the process of self-discovery and self-definition is careful inspection of what you think you should be—and according to whose laws. Accept that you are a changing, growing, kaleidoscopic person, and then use that awareness to explore and experiment.

The Third Foundation Stone:
Driving Your Own Bus

Richard Bandler began his book, *Using your Brain . . . For a Change*, with a discussion about how we have allowed ourselves to be passengers on our own bus instead of driving the bus. Instead of using our brain power . . . we let it use us.

To build a strong partnership between the conscious and unconscious mind, the steering wheel needs to be firmly in our hands. Life depends totally on us for the desired results. Nobody else can take this *responsibility* for us.

Here is another paradox. When we fully determine that our lives are in our own hands and nobody is going to play Prince Charming or fairy godmother or Peter Pan—when we really get it—life fills with a deep sense of assistance and guidance from some higher source, and we no longer feel alone. Accepting aloneness gives us a freedom from fear (of rejection or abandonment) and allows us to form connections with other human beings and with the greater powers beyond.

This is an important building block. Something awful happens when I believe that somebody out there will make it happen for me—a too common theme in advertising, magazines, and books. If I can just find the right person, job, workshop, pay scale or set of circumstances, then life will be good. Sooner or later this myth falls to pieces and stark cold reality emerges; my life is my own.

We have to drive our own bus. There is nothing out there that can give me the inner richness and zest I want.

What does that mean, exactly? Driving our own bus? Think of your body as the shell of a bus. We keep it clean and full of fuel and ready to go at any moment—that is essential. The brain and the ten senses act as the steering wheel, the clutch, and the gears, the parts of the bus that make it move.

Driving our own bus can be incredible with the proper

learning at the proper time. Do it now. Say good-bye to the fairy tales and grab that wheel. I remember how disenchanted I was when I realized that marriage was not *thee answer*, that it would not give me the things I had been taught to expect. At first I was angry, then frightened, then blaming . . . and then I began to learn to drive my own bus. And then the joy ride began.

The Fourth Foundation Stone:
If It Isn't Fun, It Isn't Worth Doing

Do you love your work? Do you wake up each morning and feel excited and alive to face the day? A major part of our adult lives will be spent working and choosing the work you love is crucial.

If we are driving our own bus, work and play should be almost synonyms. Inside all of us there exists desire, passion, and a dynamic urge to learn and create. Our talents are like rough, uncut gems and digging them out and cutting and polishing them can only be a pleasure, pure and simple.

The hard part is discovering where to dig and which gems to polish. Our work should be natural, fulfilling, and easy, not some task fobbed on us by old programming or social norms. Work should take us closer to who we want to be. Success is loving what you do—and doing what you love.

Janet Woitez, author of *Adult Children of Alcoholics* says that most of us move through life like great cons or frauds utterly fearful of the day when someone will detect the con game. Lurking in the recesses of our minds is the feeling that, "I made myself up." I remember that feeling in school. Every good grade I received on a project or paper, I'd think, "Wow, I sure pulled that one off." I secretly thought I was a fraud.

Now I understand this differently. Of course I make myself up. Now I call it personal growth. Life is all make-believe. Success is making-believe hard enough and with enough action to see results in the real world. The tricky part is to make me up in a way that gives me pleasure and depth and that follows my natural passion. I made believe that I was a writer, and then I started doing what writers do (writing words on paper). Now I am writing a book—all on the strength of my make-believe.

I meet so many people--aging adults—who are still saying "Maybe someday I will travel, go back to school, find my mate .

35

. . I say, if not now, when?

Maybe some day is just one way to avoid being all we can be, a convenient excuse, as a good friend of mine likes to call the reasons for not becoming all we can be.

What are your convenient excuses?

I have used three of the most popular convenient excuses for avoiding me—kids, money, and time. In my groups I often have people write or express what they want (really want), and I begin by not allowing them to use *money* or *time* (as in, not enough of) as an excuse for why they are not doing or having what they want.

Excuses and *maybe some day* are the real con jobs, the real fraud, the things that keep us from grabbing that steering wheel and gaining enough response-ability to create the life we want. The result of *maybe some day* is mediocrity and a fear-driven life.

Excuses won't work in this partnership of the self. Yes, it's tough to think of getting there without the convenient excuse to use as a false crutch but the excuses must leave. The truth is, getting what we want requires persistence and persevering energy, but then how much energy does it take to hold ourselves in a place we don't want to be? Excuses and justification exhaust the body when they become a way of life. Depletion and burnout are the result.

Work is work is work unless we find out what it is that fires us up and adds to who we are rather than taking away from who we are.

For example, Tammy, a beautiful and creative client, was studying algebra and accounting. She hated every minute of it.

Who is making her choices for her about what it means to "be somebody"? It was sad. She ignored who she is and chose a career that sticks her in a room alone with papers and routine work. Of course, this does not mean avoid anything that is difficult to accomplish—any road we choose is going to have its hard climbs, its unpredictable twists and turns, and its shadowy times; but why avoid the natural path and take the obstacle course instead?

We need to stay on a course of our own design, one chosen from the realm of "make-believe" buried in the hidden desires and dreams of who we are.

Again, this is where the unconscious moves in to assist us. Through the messages, the feelings, it lets us know which turns

36

to make, which fork to select, which slope to climb by sending us a gut response.

Try this. Here is a list of things for you to consider. Keep it simple and do it quickly. Check out the inner response to each item below, choosing the strongest first response.

Take a moment to slowly consider the last time you experienced each of these events and remember . . .

> . . . having a tooth filled,
> . . . a warm spring day,
> . . . your neighbor,
> . . . running out of gas,
> . . . cooking a meal for a large group,
> . . . nice cool sheets on a hot summer night,
> . . . a walk in the woods.

Notice the different responses in your body as you recall each one. That is a gut response. Of course, some tasks like going to the dentist or eating the right foods need a bit of a future orientation so that we can get the long-term response we desire (a healthy mouth, feeling good physically). However, we basically know which ones we like and which ones we dislike. Again, our body's responses are like indicator lights that lets us know WHO we are at any moment in time.

Read the list of opposite experiences below and use your gut response to learn more about what you like. Ignoring such simple things can cause life-time problems. In order to select a career that makes you more, you need to know whether you like:

> . . . working inside or outside,
> . . . with people or alone,
> . . . innovating ideas or implementing ideas,
> . . . high energy activities or low energy activities,
> . . . working with your hands or working with
> your brain?

This is such a simple checklist but, if we trust the inner response (whether for or against), we will have a baseline of information about who we are and what kind of work would be fun. Too often we ignore that initial strong response because of secondary responses about what is expected of us, what will make the most money, or what someone else tells us we should or shouldn't do. This is not driving our own bus; this is not doing what is fun.

To become all we can be is not a simple task. So many years of myths, messages, and faulty construction must be packed up and put away and the new pieces unpacked and put to work. It is an exciting process, though, and well worth the effort.

The Fifth Foundation Stone:
One Day at a Time

Life is a tough task-master when we direct all of our time and energy toward attempting to interpret the past or predict the future. Both rob us of the present moment. Life is right here, right now.

Here is an example of being present in the moment. My first NLP trainer, Tom Fairhurst, became terminally ill of liver cancer some years after our training. My first husband, Wayne, and I were close enough to Tom to name our son after him. Before Tom died, Wayne went to see him in Kansas. Wayne asked Tom how he was handling the experience of dying and he said, "As long as I separate out the past pain and the future pain—the present pain I can handle."

Tom died shortly after, refusing pain medication throughout his dying so that he wouldn't miss a single moment with his family. He did not sacrifice his "response-ability" and even wanted to experience his own death.

The present pain and discomfort are almost never more than we can bear. In fact, it is often just the right amount of discomfort we need to get moving or make a change. Emotional pain is like sandpaper—it is the friction that smoothes the wood to an elegant finish. Without life's friction, we'd remain rough lumber.

Imagine life to be in a continuous figure eight or the symbol for infinity. The past is one loop, the future is the other loop, and the present is where they intersect. Our past is a reservoir of learning and experience, and the future is like a lighthouse, a beacon to guide us in the present moment.

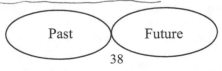

The past and future are balanced against one another as we learn to become more "response-able." We take from the past to fashion the future, but we never stay stuck in either loop.

If we are stuck in the past loop dwelling constantly on old hurts, resentments and traumatic events, everything is doomsday and our figure eight looks like this:

If we are caught in a bubble of wishful thinking about the future or longing for what is *out there*, we have built our lives around a day that never arrives and the figure eight looks like this:

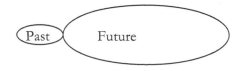

The figure eight needs graceful balance. The past and future are only reference material for this moment. Nothing more! Learning to stay in the moment comes from the constant grooming of inner awareness.

Much learning and practice must occur in order for the strength of these foundation stones to be fully realized. The commitment to grow and change will carry the movement on the infinity loop and keep us from bogging down in either the past or the future.

There is one more building block to inspect before we move into selecting the tools for creating this marvelous structure of our lives.

The Sixth Foundation Stone:
A Power Greater Than You or I

If you are like me when I first began, you may already be

thinking, "Here comes the preachy God stuff." In my youth, I arm-wrestled with God—or the concept of God that I was given. This may or may not be true for you, but we can't proceed without exploring the concept of a Higher Power.

Old belief systems around God must often be forsaken. Instead, all we need to do is accept that there is a force or power that exists in the universe that is greater than we are.

It is not difficult to find examples of a power greater than we are. For instance, you and I together are a power greater than either one of us alone. Add other powers, explained or unexplained, natural or supernatural, and we will have this sixth foundation stone in place. A "higher power" does not have to be defined in religious language. In fact, in my experience, it is impossible to define at all, except as I know it in my own being.

This greater power must be acknowledged so that there is a "power source" to draw on as we continue constructing our lives. We need a switch, an outlet, a connection with a larger source of power. If there is no spiritual connection, or no higher power—there is no reason or purpose in continuing this.

Viktor Frankl in his book, *Man's Search for Meaning,* wrote that the people who survived the Nazi concentration camps were the people who had a strong sense of purpose. So it is for us. There must be a reason for this—a purpose—even if we do not fully understand.

Organized religions have often dished out beliefs about God and our purpose that never quite fit with how we felt on the inside. Remember, we have agreed to temporarily set aside all beliefs and are sitting in our plain brown-wrapper building. We can decide what fits and what doesn't. In some instances, outdated religious training can also become a "convenient excuse" not to discover the true self or a higher power.

The experience of a higher power cannot be explained by religious or New Age language. This experience is so deeply rooted within us that it is beyond language. It is a power source that can only be mapped and discovered in personal experience.

Note: I noticed as I reentered this entire chapter that I often get lost in my own writerly thoughts. I tried to trim and cut but the "Six foundation stones" still get a bit lost in the words. For my benefit (and I hope for yours), I'll simply list them here so I can see how they look without the padding.

The Six Foundation Stones
1. Change is the only constant in life.
2. We can never be always at anything.
3. We must drive our own bus.
4. If it isn't fun, it isn't worth doing.
5. One day at a time.
6. Rely on a power greater than you or I.

Since the first printing of this book, both of my parents have passed away. My father died first. After his death my mother showed me two ragged pieces of paper that he carried in his wallet most of his adult life. My father was a tremendous influence in both my emotional and my creative life. His name was Richard Baird. I offer the quotes here, perhaps for you to put in your wallet. His quotes seem to summarize the heart of this book. The first quote was not cited. I'd love to hear from anybody who knows its source.

> "Man is buffeted by circumstances so long as he believes himself to be the creature of outside conditions, but when he realizes that he is a creative power, and that he may command the hidden soil and seed of his being out of which circumstances grow, he then becomes the rightful master of himself."
>
> --Author unknown

> "I cannot give you the formula for success, but I can give you the formula for failure which is: Try to Please Everybody."
>
> --Herbert B. Swope

41

Chapter Six
Beware the Jabberwock

Tools of the Trade

For any master craftsperson or artist the quality of the tools will determine the quality of the work. For a painter, the tools are a fine brush and high quality paints; for a carpenter, a sharp saw, a good planer and a ruler; and for a chef, a good knife and the finest beef. In this business of developing the self, what do we need to create our masterpiece?

We need a sharpened sensory awareness, response-ability, a clear understanding of the role of feelings and behaviors, and the right language. In this chapter we will look at the way we use words as tools for shaping our lives. Although the structure of language could not be covered in an entire book, we will explore a few of the most common flaws that lessen the quality of our workmanship.

A Word by Any Other Name Is Still a Word

How easy it is to have a falsely-grounded faith in language and forget its original purpose—which is to map and describe inner and outer reality. A word is only a symbol—not the experience it is attempting to describe.

Again, a word is only a *symbol*—not the *experience* it is attempting to describe.

Language often does a poor job of describing inner and outer reality. The inner world is so rich and multi-dimensional that words often fail us. In many ways words are like paper money. Money is a symbol of piles of gold locked away in Ft. Knox. Paper is used simply because gold is too awkward to haul around, but it is still only a representation of the gold in Ft. Knox.

Even more confusing, a check is a symbol of the symbolic paper money that represents the gold in Ft. Knox. Now it is two times removed from the original value of gold. Last week, you may have used your credit card that you paid with a paper check based on paper money that depends on the gold sitting

43

in Ft. Knox (now three times removed). This sounds like the house that Jack built, right? Well, language is the same way. Let's follow one experience through the same process.

Let's say that I use the word *grief* to describe the process I am going through around losing a parent. Five little letters to describe the following.

I am driving down the road and see a car that is identical to the car my father drove. The car brings to mind the funeral, which triggers a series of good memories, and I feel the sensation of love. Next my mind flips to a picture of my father in the coffin and the love dissolves back into grief. Whew. That is a bundle of complex inner experience to stuff into one tiny, five-letter word.

Words are often far removed from the actual experiences they are intended to describe. To make things even more difficult, my words go to your ears in order to communicate meaning, and now those words must run through all of your neural networks so that you can make meaning out of them. Is it any wonder that the communication process so easily breaks down?

One of the first lessons taught in NLP (Neurolinguistic Programming) is that the, "meaning of any communication is the response it gets." In other words, if the people we are communicating with are not *getting* our message—the responsibility lies with us. We are not sending clear messages.

Muddy communication is devastating. The only way to offer a clear message is to keep the sensory channels (all ten of them) uncluttered. If a rain gutter on the house fills with leaves and muck, the water runs over everywhere except down the downspout. The same is true with the communication process.

Pay attention to your sensory channels. Have you ever been driving somewhere and suddenly noticed what a gorgeous day it was or how beautiful the land is? These sensory breakthroughs are like suddenly coming awake. How easy it is to be so caught up in busy-ness that we forget to pay attention to our immediate sensory field. Remember that these ten sensory systems, five internal and five external, are our link to the universe. On these channels entire worlds are built—or crashed.

And language simply symbolizes this inner universe.

Consciously taking a moment to notice the air, any smells,

the temperature, the sights and sounds will improve these external sensory systems. To increase awareness of the inner sensory systems, meditate, relax, bathe, breathe, listen to music and pay attention to any internal images, sounds, feelings or tastes and smells. Do whatever works for you to keep those systems clear.

Getting Specific

Rule number one is to learn to get specific about what you want.

If you want to be happy, successful, joyful, creative, peaceful, animated, enthusiastic and not sad, angry, failing, depressed, fearful, anxious, begin by defining *specifically* what any of those words means to you. Again, the word is not the experience.

To get specific with language, learn to ask questions that direct and guide your answers. Below are samples of questions that can guide us toward a specific outcome. In NLP, they are known as the *Outcome Frame*. Because I like to journal, writing these out in my notebook helps me to find the desired outcome.

1. What, specifically, do I want?
   (I must be able to sense or see it).

2. How will I know when I have it?
   (What exactly will change from my current picture or sensations?)

3. What is keeping me from getting it?
   (Again, the obstacles must be visible and defined.)

4. What else will change when I have it?
   (Find specific pictures and sensations in the body.)

5. Have I ever had it?
   (A reference into the past to find similar experiences.)

6. What can I begin doing now to get it?
   (Beginning to form a specific action plan.)

45

7. Is there anything I will have to give up in order to
    have this?

These questions will lead us toward solutions—and not
toward more problems. How often have you had someone
come up to you and ask, "What's wrong? You look awful." If
you were feeling lousy to begin with, chances are you will feel
even worse by the time your *friend* is finished.

Consider the questions below in what I jokingly call the
Anti-Outcome Frame. (Please do not make a habit of using
these. Unfortunately this is the current reality of many people.)

1. What's wrong?
    (Search the brain for all bad-day experiences.)

2. How awful is it?
    (Use all bad moments to trigger more bad moments.)

3. Have you ever felt this terrible before?
    (More past referencing—look for the worst.)

4. Can life possibly get any worse?
    (Make future images of how much worse it
    could get.)

5. In how many other circumstances have you felt this
    terrible? (Even more references to past horrors.)

Language is very powerful and can lead a person in and out
of various experiences like a puppy on a leash. We have to be
very careful about creating useful experiences with the words
and tonal inflections we select.

Also, in using the Outcome Frame, stay away from the
word *why*. Asking why serves no useful purpose; why am I this
way, why was I born now, why did this have to happen to me?
People who are addicted to digging up the past are never free
to face the future. The question is how can I make it different
now or what do I really want/need here?

Without a well-built outcome, I'm a rudderless ship drifting
around the open sea. It is easy to know what it is I don't
want—but it takes real effort and energy to define what it is
that I *do* want. Here are some additional guidelines for getting

46

specific: A well built outcome:

- uses language that is specific
  (rich vs. how rich, specifically?)
- is stated positively,
- is obtainable in the real world of possibility,
- depends only on you for realization (although others may be involved in the process selected),
- adds to life and does not take away,
- is generative and spreads out in life like
- a pretty flowering vine,
- does not impact others (or the inner self) negatively.

It's not easy to discover a well-built outcome, yet it is very important. Sometimes it helps to hand a friend that list of questions and have them ask you them over and over until your ideas begin to formulate and take shape. Just for a bit of practice on designing a well-formed outcome, try the exercise below.

Exercise:

Take a sheet of paper and number it from one to ten. Split the page into two columns with the first column titled, "Things I don't want/deserve to have." Now list ten feelings or experiences you currently have but do not want to have. Sometimes it is easier to get to what we want by listing what we don't want.

Now make a second column titled, "What I want." Take each item on your list (one at a time) and use the Outcome Frame to define in positive terms what you would rather have in place of what you currently have that you don't want. For example, "I do not deserve to be constantly criticized." becomes "I am gentle and respectful toward myself and do not allow myself to be criticized inappropriately." Or "I am strong and confident and teach others how to treat me respectfully."

The key to using this successfully is to create a clear internal image or a mental movie with sounds, feelings, and pictures where you can see and feel your outcome as real.

Now ask the question, "What keeps me from having that?"

47

and then listen carefully to your inner response.

Here is an example of why a desired change sometimes doesn't happen. Susan wanted to lose weight. When the question, "Is there anything I will have to give up in order to have this?" came up, she realized that the friends she had, the man she'd married, even her work had been chosen based on being overweight. If Susan's weight problem went away, it was possible that everything else in her life would change. She had to check out her willingness to make any other changes that could come with losing weight.

It is amazing how few of us have really sat and thought about the person we want to become. During a client session, I asked Joe, "Imagine you could have anything that you wanted . . . there are absolutely no obstacles standing in your way. Anything you desire is suddenly available. What would you want?"

He thought for a long, long time, and finally said, "Well, I would really like some camping gear."

I offered him the sun and the moon—and he took one grain of sand from the beach. Often, we're far too short-sighted about what we want.

Again and again I have said to a room full of people, "Where would you like to be five or ten years from now? Imagine that anything is possible and there are no obstacles." Again and again people imagine only a mild modification of what they already have. We lack vision and a future orientation.

On the other hand, sometimes what we think we want is not *really* what we want. I may say I want a million dollars when what I really want is the *time* that cool million would buy me; time to play, write, create . . . . The real desired outcome is the freedom to pursue my dreams.

One time I sat and wrote down the twenty things I most loved doing. When I finished, I realized that out of the twenty items, only three required any money at all. The rest only required the free time to do them. There is a saying that goes, "Do what you love and the money will follow." For me, this has been true.

Besides practicing and working with the Outcome Frame questions, carefully study the language traps outlined in the next few pages. Each linguistic trap can become a barrier that keeps us from getting what we want and deserve to have.

A second exercise is to simply take a notebook and begin writing the Outcome Frame questions again and again, repeating "What do I really want?" When the mind tosses up an answer like, "I want money," keep writing and ask more questions such as, "And if I had money, then I would have . . . what?"

The Non-Sense Words

In general, we give words too much importance and power. Like paper and plastic money, words are without value unless we can specifically and fully imagine them with our ten senses.

In Genie LaBourde's book, *Influencing with Integrity,* she talks about what she calls "fat" words. These are vague, padded, chubby words that sound great but mean nothing. Fat words cannot be located specifically in the senses. Examples are words like love, peace, security, wealth, satisfaction, depression, fear, serenity, sadness, success, failure, happiness etc, etc. Fat words have no sensory base and are, therefore, *non-sense.* Fat words have no sensation, motion, sound, taste, smell or image attached to them.

A fat word has attempted to become a noun (people, place or thing). However, they cannot be held, touched, tasted, or seen. They are not things. We can't own them.

The technical term for a fat word is a *nominalization.* They are I that have lost their "ing" endings and become static. In reality, when we add the "ing" endings we get more specific action words like playing and giggling and touching and weeping and risking and reaching and stretching and crying and on and on in perpetual motion.

Is it any wonder that a beautiful set of actions denoted by the phrase "I *love* you" often turns into "I own you"? When someone is *loving* you, they are chatting and smiling and whispering and touching and . . . well, you get my message. Fat words are just fat words unless there is motion, endless motion.

For example, I can ask you to *trust* me, but at this point you cannot have the faintest idea what that means in terms of how you should act toward me. Trust is simply a symbol of a process and unless you ask for more specific information, you remain clueless. Every individual has a separate definition of the process of *trusting.* We assume that we share a common definition, but we cannot know this unless we ask.

49

Success, the ultimate brass ring, in reality means sweaty palms and pounding hearts and shaking knees. If you aren't involved in some challenging series of motions, then it isn't *success*. Succeeding is the constant state of challenging and stretching your own ability.

We can train our ears to listen for fat words that promise plenty—and then we can learn to ask what that word means specifically. To turn a fat word into a lean word, get specific and force it back into actual sensory experience. Try adding "ing" to put the action back into the words: succeeding, loving, trusting. A process is not a thing (noun). Trim the fat off until you know specifically what each word represents in your inner reality.

Shoulding on Yourself

Another linguistic pitfall is use of the words should, could, must, have to, can't, always, never, and maybe. In linguistics these are called modal operators. They "operate on" our reality.

Words are meant to define and describe reality, not create it. All of these words represent hidden agendas, old belief systems, or rules that constrict our lives. These words erupt out of some dictator who lives in our heads. For example, what is something that you tell yourself when you make a mistake? "I *should* have known better than that, I can't believe I *could* be so stupid. I *must* be a fool." Can you hear all the linguistic traps? No wonder we move from feeling bad to terrible in just a few moments.

Rules must be carefully tailored to fit us. Here is a shift that is not easy to make—every part of your reality is created by you. I have heard many say, "Wait a minute, I didn't choose to be born into the family I was born into, I didn't choose my IQ, I didn't choose poverty."

Here is the hard part. You may not have chosen poor luck initially—but if it continues, you are choosing it now.

This is difficult to accept, but it is the only way to get that steering wheel back in hand and quit letting the world drive our bus around. The musts, shoulds, and maybes place the power for life in somebody else's hands. Challenge these linguistic patterns vigorously.

"I *have* to go to the store."

50

Says who?

"I *should* call Mary today."

Who says I should?

"I *can't* right now, but *maybe* when the kids are all in school I will . . . write that book start that business, go to school."

Why not now?

Modal operators (the should and coulds) are echoes of old programming, rules put in place by somebody else—not you. Examine them ruthlessly!

The Polarity Person

Some of us have a strong reaction to words like should, must, and have to—all those subtle and not-so-subtle commands. We have what is known as a polarity response. Like rebellious teenagers, we continually resist the rules and do the opposite of what is suggested. If you are this type of person, your unconscious may be using these tactics to get you to move into action.

For example, I'm a polarity person and when my inner voice whispers sarcastically "You will never amount to anything," I get angry and will do anything to prove that voice wrong. I'm immediately back in action. This can be a useful response as long as I don't start truly believing what that inner voice is saying.

Recently, I had a client who was experiencing this pattern; the demanding inner voice was really getting to him. I asked how he would react if his unconscious gently whispered to him to become everything he could be, instead of screaming and *shoulding* at him? He smiled and said that he probably would not pay attention to the gentle approach.

If the whisper doesn't work, the sarcastic shout often does. The unconscious mind uses whatever works to get our attention. Often just letting that inner voice know that we are on to the game alters the pattern, especially when we begin to pay attention to what our real needs are and respond to them quickly.

Are you a polarity person? If someone tells you that you *should* do something, do you immediately have the desire to do the opposite? Or have you ever told yourself, "I really should

51

get this house cleaned," only to feel immediate resistance to doing it?

This polarity response may be a left over from the normal process of separating from your parents and beginning to identify yourself. The parent tells the teen to stay away from so and so—and the teen is suddenly going steady with that forbidden person. This process of self-definition is natural, but we also need to understand that its early intention was to help us define our boundaries and determine who we are. It can become a problem if we are not aware of a polarity response. For example, if I think I should pay my car insurance, but I have a polarity response and *don't* pay the insurance, I could get into a fix. Many immature patterns of procrastination result from this.

We need to be clear about who we are and what we want and ride with that. Everything else may be old programming and worth discarding..

It is heartbreaking to see how many people never do tune into the deeper unconscious mind to discover what richness is there. Check out the rules, check out your language patterns, start paying attention to the familiar feelings and questioning what is really happening.

Note: Once again I have the urge to mention Robert Fritz and the concept of structural conflict. This is another explanation for many of our polarity responses. Sometimes I feel forced to choose between two equally strong but opposing desires. If I choose one, a tension instantly forms and I want the other. If you feel this conflict, do check out his books. I particularly like *The Path of Least Resistance*.

It is difficult to be cleaning up this book and resisting the urge to begin rewriting the whole thing. The sections above barely scratch the surface of linguistics and how language patterns can drive thought and behavior. Be sure to look further into it if this interests you.

There Is No They

An all too familiar pattern in people is the tendency to blame what isn't working on others. They did it . . . if they wouldn't have . . . .

Using too many pronouns that point to others (and not to

me) will keep me stuck in a blaming pattern.

I remember during a dark point in my life, I blamed the entire mess of my life on him. I honestly thought that if my first husband were more sensitive, more this or that, less this or that, my life would be better. Actually, he had nothing at all to do with my unhappiness. When our marriage counselor pointed this out, I was angry with her at first. Couldn't she see how wronged I was? Couldn't she hear what he was doing to me?

As I look back to that time, that counselor gave me a great gift . . . she gave me back my own life and power.

Exercise:

Here is an exercise to help you shift from a blame frame into an "I" frame. Scan several situations in your life that you tend to blame on others. Write them down and then switch pronouns. Be willing to ask, "How have I created or contributed to this?"

He did it >> I did it.

If she wouldn't have . . . >> If I wouldn't have . . .

When they do . . . >> When I do . . .

Even the "its" can be turned into "I statements".

It is not fair. >> I am not fair.

It should have been me. >> I should have been me.

It was meant to happen. >> I was meant to happen.

I once heard the expression, "We teach the world how to treat us." This is so true. When I blame others, I invite defense. As long as long as somebody else is at fault, I never have to be responsible for my own life.

Another way to view this is to consider that the qualities we dislike in others are a reflection of what we dislike in ourselves.

Criticism from other people only hurts when it matches self-criticism.

For instance, if someone told you that your hair was an ugly green and purple, would you feel criticized? Of course not— because you know it isn't true. But if somebody tells you that you are inadequate and stupid, it hurts because you *secretly believe* that about yourself.

The world is a mirror of inner life. Look around. What do you see? A friend once remarked, "If you want to know what your belief systems are, look at your immediate environment." Is it ordered or chaotic, rich or poor, happy or miserable, supportive or lonely, quiet or loud, unified or conflicting? Be honest in this assessment.

People in our lives also reflect inner space. If the people closest to me are critical and abusive, then this is an indicator that I am critical and abusive to the self. If the people around me are gentle and supportive, then I am gentle and supportive to the self.

Who are the people in your life? Are your closest relationships enriching or impoverishing?

When the world is placed in proper perspective, it becomes a classroom of the self. The greatest university is constantly at hand for learning more about the self. Blaming others or blaming circumstances and events (past or present) is a losing proposition.

Stop. Look. Listen. Feel. Life is a choice and we are making it now.

Something new happens as we fully enter a partnership with the inner self. Such a relationship is a gift, a glow of self-appreciation that begins to fill every empty corner of the being as each feeling is inspected and new behaviors selected. We have just spent some time inspecting the language we use daily, now what about the behaviors?

Chapter Seven
The Behavior is not the Problem

Behavior vs. Need

Just as there are linguistic traps there are similar traps in how we perceive our actions and behaviors. The presenting problems or behaviors are seldom—if ever—the real problem. For example, a family may seek help for a disruptive teenager (the presenting problem) only to find out that the real problem is how the whole family system is operating. Perhaps mom and dad are not dealing with their relationship and the teen acts out to keep the focus on him—and to keep mom and dad together.

Behaviors may appear to be random patterns but they are actually complex structures directly tied to inner need. We can only understand the behavior when we understand the need behind it. The behavior is an attempt to meet a need.

To keep it simple, we can assume that we have only a few basic physical and emotional needs that are essential to maintaining life. Once we separate the behavior from the need it is hiding, then we can generate other ways to satisfy the need.

The range and combination of behaviors are infinite. The needs, however, are finite and essential to our existence. To survive on the planet we basically need . . .

. . . to be loved and nurtured,

. . . to be fed, sheltered and safe,

. . . to self-express, or self-actualize.

This is a very simple picture of the wide range of human needs, but essentially we have an emotional body, a physical body, and a spiritual body. All three need tending and care.

The A-Frame of Need

To show how these three needs create a literal web of behaviors, look at the simple chart below of our three primary needs.

55

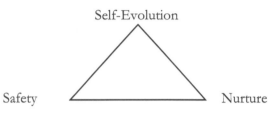

Self-Evolution

Safety   Nurture

Notice that self-evolution sits at the top. Like Maslow's theory of self-actualization, we can't fully satisfy this higher need until the bodily needs are met. It is impossible to contemplate the greater questions when the belly is rumbling or the cold is threatening—although it is our nature to always reach.

A need is something that is necessary for survival of human life. When scarcity of any need exists, we are in danger and become anxious (even desperate). Like our feelings, needs cannot be judged as good or bad. They just are. You need them in order to survive.

As we go through individual feelings later, keep the A-frame in mind; there are three primary needs and all behaviors and feelings spin off of these three needs in some way.

For instance, many of my clients have talked to me about their desire to increase their income—more money. The desire for money itself says nothing about which need may be begging for attention. I may need money to pay for heat and electricity (safety), to have people see me as successful and important (love/nurture) or to buy myself time to write the great American novel. Just saying I want money does not clarify which need is presenting.

Earlier we went through the questions designed to point you toward your desired outcome. Being clear about our needs is an important part of this process.

The goal here is to simplify the process of slicing through behaviors and getting straight to the real need. The million-dollar question is, "How do I know when a behavior is trying to tell me that a need has been unmet?

Behind Every Behavior is a Good Intention

In NLP, we are taught that behind *every* behavior there is a good intention. In other words, every behavior is attempting to satisfy a need. Every behavior has a good intention for us.

Think about that. That is the essence of this book.

Think of the cranky child having a tantrum. His intention is to gain something from a parent or adult. If we think about the triad of our basic needs listed above, the child is probably needing a) food or rest, b) attention or c) time to play and explore. He doesn't understand how to sort out what he needs and frustration leads to tantrum. The behavior results from the need. Behaviors send a message about what we need. We need to decode the messages.

From here on, we will be focusing on the *intention* behind unwanted behaviors and feelings. Personally, my most powerful personal changes have come from learning to appreciate even my most negative feelings and behaviors because I know that they are attempting to help me grow.

Just as the physical body will send symptoms to get your attention, the emotional body sends symptoms of stress, anger, sadness, and loneliness to call attention to need.

For example, when I get caught up in the day-to-day grind of life and am not creating, I get depressed. I want to sleep or eat or feel angry. What makes more sense? To pay attention to the depression—or to get back to creating?

Or suppose I am feeling overwhelmed and alone, and I pick a fight with my husband to get his attention (like a child's tantrum). How successfully have I taken care of the need to feel more connected?

By setting aside the behaviors and concentrating on the need, I am more likely to satisfy the need and the behavior will change naturally. For example, suppose I am having one of those days when I feel all alone in the world, like nobody loves me or cares that I exist. I feel scared. My choices are to react to the fear with negative behaviors or to probe the need itself and satisfy that.

A startling thing happens when you really understand that behaviors direct us to hidden needs. Suddenly we realize that we are all just attempting to get our needs met in a confusing and complex world. We gain empathy, compassion and tolerance for ourselves and others.

The behaviors are never the real problem. Unsatisfied needs must be met in order to survive. People do need people, but they need themselves and the ability to respond first.

To change behaviors we need more (and better) choices on

57

how to meet our needs. More choice is the critical phrase here. It takes time and energy to widen the range of choices we have for meeting needs when old patterns of behavior have ceased to work. In the chapter to follow we look at the smaller pieces of inner awareness with the intention of fine-tuning our ability to respond.

To gain the most from the remainder of this book, read slowly and take the time to discover how each of your behaviors is connected to a need.

Chapter Eight:
What Does Inner Awareness Mean?

Submodalities: The Tiny Chunks of Awareness

So far, we have looked at belief systems, language patterns, and now behavior patterns. We are still sitting in our plain-wrapper structures looking into our patterns with more and more awareness of how the human brain builds experiences. These are the basics for the study of the self that we need to continue forward. Understanding how we construct our map of the world allows us greater choices on how to *act* rather than *react* to trigger experiences.

Earlier, I talked about the importance of the five senses of touch, taste, smell, sound, and sight as the vehicles for gaining information about the world. It is the information coming in on these sensory channels that stimulates the brain and causes all of the wonderful chemical and electrical exchanges known as thinking, learning, and emoting.

Many of these exchanges are still a mystery even to the scientific world. I cannot begin to give you the *how it works* of the human brain. Instead, we can become more aware of the information sifting around in the senses and learn what to do with it.

In an earlier discussion, I made a distinction between inner and outer awareness stating that the five senses are actually ten. Five are for recording and sorting the outside world and five are for recording and sorting the inside world. The technology known as Neurolinguistic Programming defines each sense as a *modality* and then breaks each modality into smaller bits called *submodalities*. The language is new and confusing but is worth the time it takes to learn it because it gives us a new set of tools for analyzing the way we put our inner lives together.

The sensory channels we will deal most directly with here are the visual, auditory, and kinesthetic (touch) modalities. For example, you receive images in your mind via the visual modality. On closer examination of these pictures, you will discover that there are tiny, but observable, distinctions within each internal picture. These are called submodality distinctions. Noticing these sub-modality differences and learning to work with them can put the choice for change in your hands.

We'll go through the three primary sensory modalities with examples in order to give you a fuller understanding of how to work with the tiny pieces of our sequences.

Visual Submodalities

Everybody has pictures in their heads except, perhaps, a person who has been blind from birth. Some people are more consciously aware of these pictures, some less aware, depending on which sensory system he or she relies on most heavily. These inner pictures often have a profound influence on how we experience each moment. They can, in fact, drive our emotions and behaviors. When triggered, a phobic fear or the memory of a traumatic experience can cause the remembered pictures, sounds, and feelings to rush up close and surround us. It is so quick that there seems to be no time/space distance to allow us to act rather than react. The sensation is big and overwhelming.

In order to control the fear or the bad memory, we have to slow it down and notice how that memory is stored in the brain. The brain's very innocent intention is to make sure we do not experience the trauma again. It is warning us—but the warning becomes the primary response and instead of avoiding the past, we re-experience it.

With practice and response-ability, we can begin to catch finer and finer distinctions in these pictures, and even learn to arrange and rearrange at will. Here are several examples of visual submodality distinctions. You may want to recall some ordinary moment and test out each submodality against the inner picture.

Brightness: Is the picture bright, dim, hazy, fizzy, high light or low light?

Size: Is the picture larger than life, life-size or tiny and diminished in size?

Color/black and white: Are the pictures in full color, shades of grey, partial coloring or black and

60

white?

Location: Notice whether the pictures are "right before your eyes" or located in unusual relationship to you.

Distance: Are the pictures close to you or distant and far away?

Clarity: Are the images sharply defined, or fuzzy and grainy in appearance? Do they sparkle? Are they dull?

Motion/still life: Do you see only single still frames like photographs or do full length movies run through your mind?

Speed: How fast or slow are the images moving?

Frame size/ panoramic: Are the pictures enclosed in a frame or do they appear panoramic?

Sequence: Are the movies in order or is there a confetti effect, several pictures simultaneously flashing?

Associated/dissociated: Can you see yourself in the picture (dissociated) or is it like seeing out of your own eyes again (associated)?

Those are only a few of the quality distinctions possible. The key is to pay attention.

Begin by imagining several simple scenes, perhaps breakfast this morning, last week's walk by the river, a fairly pleasant memory? Go through that list and jot down any distinctions you notice.

Now, try a mildly unpleasant memory, a contest of will with the boss, a tense exchange with a weary child. (Save the more painful memories for later, after you have practiced.) Again, jot down any distinctions you notice. Now compare the two lists. Are there any quality differences between the pleasant and

61

unpleasant memories?

Now, here is a real test of your talents. Try moving the pictures up closer or further away or adding and subtracting color or brightness. Change the frame size from large to small or small to large. As you play with this, notice any differences in how the adjustments *feel* to you. Can you make the pleasant memory even more pleasant? Can you *fade out* the unpleasant memory like a television fade? This may seem like a simple task, but if the feelings shifted, you have just managed to change your own memory.

Change can be fun. I once heard a statement that impressed me, although I can't recall its origins now. It said, "There is absolutely no pain in change . . . only in resistance to change."

Note: The visual modality is well used by athletes, salespeople, and others who hope to bring about a success-ful or prosperous outcome. Although I don't like to see this trivialized, you actually are much more likely to travel in the right direction if you can see clearly—and up close—what you want to achieve.

Auditory Submodalities

In our modern world, the visual modality (and submodalities) seems to get a lot of credit for manifesting success and prosperity. The auditory modality, on the other hand, often gets a bad rap. Hearing voices in your head is not always well received. However, we all have sound tracks running. Like pictures, we have sounds, voices, tape loops stored in our brains. How we use them is just as important as learning to work with inner pictures. I can almost guarantee that a person with "low self esteem" is, in fact, spending a lot of time berating themselves in the auditory system. He or she is surely recounting every screw up, using a negative tone of voice, and saying nasty things about the Self. Imagine listening to "You stupid, dumb son of a bitch. Can't you do anything right?" over and over again. What would happen to your self-esteem?

Here are just a few of the auditory quality differences or submodalities to notice. As in the earlier list, recall an actual recent conversation with someone and then do the same thing with something you say to yourself on a regular basis. Listen

62

carefully and compare as we go through these.

Volume: How loud or soft are the words you hear internally?

Speed: Do the words come in a rush? Or very . . . slow . . . and . . . deliberate?

Location: Which ear do you hear the words in? Do they come from in front of you or behind you or above you?

Distance: Do you hear the words very close to you or distant and diminished as if they are coming from the next room?

Tonal: What is the tonal quality? Is it soothing or harsh? Is it your voice or does it resemble someone else's voice (a parent, teacher, etc.)

Pitch: Is the voice pitched very high, low or mid-range?

Experiment with these quality differences just like you did with the pictures. Try it first with a conversation you may have had with another person. And then do the same with something you say to yourself when you are pleased with a task well done or with a problem you recently solved by thinking it through. Jot down the submodality differences.

Now, think of the last time you made a mistake or embarrassed your self somehow. What did you say to yourself about that incident? Again, jot down the quality differences from the list above. It may take a little practice to begin to notice these, especially if the auditory system is not one you most commonly pay attention to, but it does get easier with practice.

Now make some changes in the qualities of that internal voice. What happens if you speed either memory up like a fast record? Or make the pitch abnormally high and squeaky? Try changing both memories by running through the list of quality differences and noticing any changes in your experiences. Many people chuckle when I have them hear the self-criticism in a whiney, nasal voice or imagine hearing it in Donald Duck or Mickey Mouse's voice. It just doesn't pack the same punch, does it?

Again, when you have successfully changed these subtle submodalities, you have come one step closer to driving your own bus. There is so much talk about self-concept and self-esteem and other fat words but, in reality, most of us walk around talking to ourselves in the nastiest voice possible. If you wouldn't use that tone of voice on a loved one—or even a total stranger—don't use it on yourself. Practice changing the quality of your inner voice.

Kinesthetic Submodalities

Kinesthetic is the word commonly given to the sense of touch. It includes physical movement and sensation, intuition, gut responses, and assorted feelings. You probably notice in the pieces above, that your reactions to the pictures or words were measured by how you *felt* about them. This is your kinesthetic system operating. And like with the visual and auditory systems, the kinesthetic system also has subtle submodality distinctions. Here are a few. Pick a simple experience, like petting a dog or experiencing a mild fear as you read through the list.

Pressure: Do you feel pressure or a sense of being pushed down or away from something?

Location: Where in your body are various sensations located? In the midsection? Head? Limbs?

Motion: Is there a sense of movement (tingling, tickling, heaviness, beehive activity or butterflies)?

Temperature: What parts of the body feel hot or cold or damp at different moments in time?

Intensity: What part of the body receives the greatest intensity of sensation?

Pace: Is there a feeling of racing or of time... being... slowed... down?

Associated/dissociated: Do you feel like you are reliving the experience or do you feel like it is happening to someone else, as if you are watching it?

Of course, in the kinesthetic modality, (as well as the others) remember that there are internal and external influences happening all the time or sequences between the modalities with one triggering responses in another. Have you ever walked into a room and smelled a scent that reminded you of your grandmother's house and that scent triggered old memories complete with pictures, words, and feelings? This would be one of those triggered sequences.

Now, for some additional practice, think of a time recently when you were real excited about something—perhaps a pay raise, a visit from a close friend or a baby's first word. Run through all of the submodalities for visual, auditory and kinesthetic systems and notice the specific qualities of that state of excitement, especially where in your body you experience them. Jot them down on a piece of paper.

Now select a memory that was mildly fearful to you, a car cut out in front of you or a rumored lay off at work. Check each item on the list, noticing any quality differences and jot them down. Where do you feel this fear? What does it feel like?

What are the quality differences between fear and excitement? How can you tell one from the other? Now try changing each submodality by moving the feelings around or changing the intensity or temperature of it. Once again, when you alter the sensation, you alter the way it is being experienced in the moment.

I could do the same with taste and smell, but these are lesser used systems, and I think you now have a fair idea of what we are doing. Don't ignore taste and smell as these can be powerful triggers.

In the next few chapters, we will be exploring many aspects of the self. Using this wonderfully detailed information as you move through the pages and patterns will be a significant help to you. We want to bring our level of awareness up—way up. These tiny submodality distinctions will help you become aware of and even change patterns of behavior and experience. If you ignore the tiny pieces, there is little hope for the larger pieces.

Big fat words like depression, procrastination, grief or fear are just long combinations and sequences of these smaller stored submodality pieces triggered by some outside experience. When lumped together into one tangled mess, they become dis-ease and dis-comfort.

Before moving fully into the construction phase, I want to include one more tool that will help keep all of these tiny pieces from jumbling together. This tool becomes the guide or the teacher—an overseer of the entire production crew. Remember that popular comment about "It's hard to drain the swamp when you're up to your eyeballs in alligators"? Well, this is where you learn to tame the alligators so you can drain the swamp.

Creating the Internal Overseer

We all have moments when we need to take counsel with a person wiser or more experienced than ourselves. That is just good sense. However, we often develop a pattern of never trusting the self to provide the answers. It becomes a bad habit to always ask others for the right answers to our important questions. What is right for them may not be right for me. I am the only one who lives in my body.

The seminar/lecture business is a multi-billion dollar a year industry. I've met many people who spend a great deal of time and money searching for the *one* with the right answers-- seminar junkies on a steady diet of self-help.

Why do we do this? Because we don't have enough tools to sort it out for ourselves. Wouldn't it be wonderful to develop an internalized part of yourself who could answer the questions, and then begin learning to trust that part? Well, that is the goal here.

All good teachers eventually work themselves out of a job. If a person has been your teacher and you have learned the lessons presented, you will lose your need of his or her services. The teacher is now an internalized part of you. However, too often we become dependent on the teacher and never learn to trust the inner self.

Think of it like this. Imagine a loop of energy or power coming out of you and reaching out to another person like an umbilical cord. The person answers the question or fills the need and the loop returns to you. It is a *gestalt* or a completed loop.

That is good, right? In fact, that is what human relationships are all about, but what happens when that person disappoints you, dies, or moves to California? What then? Your loop has a gaping hole in it and you feel abandoned or lost.

We often become overly dependent on a spouse, or a teacher, therapist or even a close friend and it works well—until they leave.

Now imagine that there is a part of *you* on the opposite end of your loop, and that the energy runs out from you, is served by that other part of you and then returns to you intact. There is no chance of that part disappointing you or leaving. The internal guide is yours to keep forever.

It is too easy to place trust in another human being, and forget that he is just that—another human being, with all the human flaws and fallacies inherent in the race.

How do you build this internal teacher, an overseer that you can trust to provide insight and answers in times of need? It requires practice, but is quite simple to do. We all have deep reservoirs of resources we can draw on and trust if we only learn to access them. Most of the information you need is already within in the form of our own senses, behaviors, and needs. We just need a little practice and know-how in order to access it.

When I first went into business for myself, I felt lost without a boss and found it difficult to stay on track. To overcome this, I created an idea of myself ten years down the road who was highly successful, and then I let her--the future me—guide me in the moment. Naturally, she didn't have all of the answers, but she was better at asking the right questions and wasn't as insecure.

To choose a guide or an internal overseer, begin by spending a few minutes alone in a quiet place. Relax and imagine yourself at one of your favorite places, a creek or a hillside perhaps, or design a beautiful room that is just for you. Make sure that it is a place that feels safe and pleasant to you. Now place yourself in that special place and get to know it. When you are at ease, imagine another person joining you. This may be someone you know and respect, a person who guided you through tough times or perhaps a person you want to be more like or who has personal qualities you admire. Like my internal boss, this person can even be a future you.

Remember that you are dipping into your own unconscious mind for this special guide. I have had many clients report that a name (not a person they even know) came immediately to mind or that they had a complete image and personality already formed when they sought it. One of the mysteries, I guess, but do not be surprised if you get very clear idea of your inner guide. The unconscious mind may be very ready and willing to work with you on this.

Once we have selected the Internal Overseer, practice being with him or her, asking questions and listening for the answers. We might hear the answers or get an image or a scene that somehow answers the questions. This may not even be a person but more an intuitive sense of knowing. Remember that this is just information coming from the wiser parts of our own being. Pay careful attention to the submodality distinctions we went through earlier.

When you have practiced working with your internal overseer, you can eventually begin to access it on the go. One of the problems with many meditation techniques is they become unavailable—unless you are meditating. We want to learn to meditate on our feet. We need techniques for getting answers in the daily hustle of life. To do this, we need to place a little time and space between us and the event we are attempting to deal with.

When In Doubt—Step Back

The first step to altering old, non-useful patterns is to practice gaining distance or stepping back from the moment. I introduced this slightly in the submodalities section above. Remember the associated position (being in the picture) and dissociated position (seeing yourself in the picture). To dissociate, practice picking a scene, noticing first of all whether you are in the picture or seeing yourself in the picture. If you are in it, take a big breath and imagine yourself stepping out of your own body and backing away until you can see yourself in the scene. If there is an age difference between you in the present moment and you in the memory, reinforce to yourself that you are older and have more skills than that younger part. It is important to stay your present age when looking into the past.

Some of us will find this easier to do than others depending upon our natural patterns. Now, to refine the skill, practice seeing yourself from every corner of the room, from the ceiling, from in front and behind. This gets easier and easier with practice. If you don't see pictures very well, just get the feeling of pulling away. One woman found it useful to imagine seeing the scene as if it were reflected in a mirror.

This added distance, called a meta-position, lends clarity to the scene and gives you time to consult with the overseer. When you feel more distant from the scene ask, "What do I need in this situation, and what possible responses or solutions are available to me?" Your overseer will help you come up with the best possible choices, and then you can step back in and respond. Once you have practiced stepping out into this new perspective and then stepping back in to the scene again, try it on a tougher event. If you are having trouble, separate even further by asking "What does *she* need to do?" Separating your pronouns (from me or my—to she or her) sets up one more level of dissociation.

Try it now. Think of the last time you had a major conflict, when you could really feel the push/pull or were overwhelmed with your feelings. Now, as soon as you feel that sensation of push/pull, remember that the feeling is a messenger from the unconscious and a signal to you to act.

Take a nice deep breath, and feel yourself stepping out into the meta-position and gaining distance from the scene—as far back as you need to. Yes, that's right. Back up until you can see yourself clearly in the scene. Good. You will probably notice that the sensations become less intense as you gain distance from the event. That is what you want to accomplish with this step. In the meta-position you are better able to access that store of information you have been building for years and years. You are a resourceful and adult person and creative at finding solutions to the conflict. Here is a brief outline of the steps with an example:

1. A stimulus presents itself . . .
   (Someone is critical of you or you become fearful or uncomfortable about something.)

2. You notice the message from the unconscious

69

(Your gut tightens up, throat becomes dry.)

3. Take a deep, cleansing breath or two . . .

4. Feel yourself step out in the meta-position.
   Back away until you see yourself in the scene
   and stay your present age without flipping into the
      younger self. Also be sure to see the other person if
   this memory is about someone else.

5. Ask the Overseer what is needed in this situation . . .
   (What do I need most here? What do I want?)

6. Keep asking questions until you get four or five
   different responses you could choose from. . .
   (Use humor? Be sensitive about the other person's
   day? Keep quiet? Speak up?)

7. Select the best choice. Always try to preserve the
   relationship if possible
   (Gently ask him about his day.)

8. Step back into the scene with the new choice.

9. ACT!
   (You seem a bit pent up. How was your day?)

This process is well worth practicing and perfecting. To spend life constantly reacting and never really choosing the action is unrewarding. Let yourself develop flexibility and curiosity in your actions.

Just reacting turns us into robots. Judging the event, name-calling, lashing out, and blaming only serve to make the situation deteriorate further. The only thing we are concerned with is what is the best action to resolve this conflict and maintain our integrity and good feelings about ourselves? It is seldom useful to lash out with the first words that come to mind—nobody wins in that kind of communication! There are usually many, many choices we could select from if we just took a moment to discover what they are.

It is important to practice this in order to keep a clear head when clarity is needed. I remember a friend telling me about driving up on the scene of a horrible car accident. He

70

immediately went into action, taking charge on behalf of the wounded victims. Later, he could recall the odd sensation of seeing himself doing each task quickly and efficiently while simultaneously planning the next move. He was awed by his own effectiveness in that crisis.

The key to his effectiveness was his ability to dissociate, or step away from the scene to get the larger scope of what needed to be done and to step away from any immediate feelings he was having about the horror of the moment. He was also able to respond quickly with first aid techniques that he could scarcely recall even learning. Amazing.

This is so useful in times of need. Imagine consciously choosing when to take the meta-position and when to stay in your own feelings. This is when we are truly driving our own bus.

One word of caution, however; there are people in the world who have learned to adapt by staying dissociated almost entirely, seeing themselves live their own lives, and robbing themselves of the pleasurable moments as well as the painful moments. These people have little or no expression. We sometimes call them poker faces, icebergs or stone-faces. That is not a desirable goal.

There are also people who continually replay past painful times as if they were happening in this moment, but experience all the good memories from a meta-position. Common examples of this might be people with terrible fears and phobias or victims of trauma (Vietnam veterans, or rape and abuse victims). These people need to learn when to step out and how to stay out. If the memories are too severe, you may need assistance from a specialist in NLP or a qualified counselor.

Those two types, overly dissociated or associated, are extremes. Balance in anything is good, and the meta-position or consulting the overseer is helpful whenever there is fear, nervousness, anger, grief, etc. It even helps in public speaking or important interviews to take that meta-position to remain more calm and effective. Definitely take the associated position for remembering or newly experiencing rich, pleasurable moments. These are the gifts that life yields when asked. Bring them into your sensory field as close as possible.

It may have become obvious by now that this book is about

71

action—not just reading—and that you must become an active participant. That is one problem with self-help books; they are just as easy to shelve as they are to read. It helps to buy a little notebook and start logging and tracking some of the information coming in on the senses, both inside and out. Seeing your experiences and practice in black ink on a white page can only give the details more clarity. Sensory awareness is a way of life, a road we travel every day, not a shot in the arm to get us through the lonely night.

We cannot avoid our own development and many changes. We have a binding contract called life that demands growth, no matter what we try to do to stop it.

Chapter Nine:
Emoting is not a Dirty Word

The Function of Feelings

By separating the behaviors from the needs and tracking the subtle submodalities, we may realize that the true purpose of human emotion has been misplaced. It is as though emotions have become the villains in a melodrama. Remember earlier when I talked about how there are no good or bad feelings and how tired I was of the smiling positive mental attitude people and their good feelings? Let's take an even closer look now at the function of feelings and emotions, and what could have given them such a bad name.

Have you ever felt like nobody in the whole world loved you, only to have someone say "Oh, don't be so silly. Of course you are loved."? Your feeling was discounted the same way a curious child gets a hand swatted when in danger of hurting himself. No-no, mustn't touch! But a feeling is not a hot stove, a high climb, or a busy street. And we are no longer small children in need of protection. Feelings are signals, the signs of need rising, and no-no to feelings is inappropriate. How many times have you seen someone in tears and, through the sadness, heard self-critical words like "I feel so stupid for crying. I am such a baby."

Feelings are not criminals lurking in a dark alley waiting to spring and do us harm. Feelings aren't the dark evil ones that have to be locked away behind bars and fed bread and water. In fact, feelings are our most trusted friends.

A pure feeling, congruently expressed, is always a thing of beauty and not ugliness. I am more comfortable with a dark angry look when someone is angry than a smooth, stiff smile masking the anger. A mask covering the true feeling is confusing and makes me wonder where I stand. It is incongruent and dishonest.

Double messages are when the expressions, body or tonal qualities are saying one thing and the words are saying another. For the most part, we are all lousy liars. Most people can read the truest reaction no matter the words. Double messages are highly destructive.

It takes great courage to make our inner feelings line up with what others see. We have to risk a lot. If I show you my true feelings, you may discount me—or not like me. You may tell me not to feel that or say that or be that. You might even (god forbid) give me advice on who I should be, or could be, or need to be. If I have not clearly defined myself, I'm vulnerable to your approval or disapproval.

I remember thinking my inner world was like a private a rose garden, pretty and protected. My worst fear was that I would let you enter that private place and you would come crashing in and destroy it. It frightened me. I kept it very hidden and let only a chosen few see it. Now I realize that the only way I can keep my inner courtyard beautiful is to risk sharing it with others. I need to know that emoting and expressing my self are not dangerous things.

When we learn to respond congruently to the inner self and act accordingly, life gains purpose and meaning and our relationships gain in quality.

Congruency is a match between the inner response (the private courtyard) and the outward expression or action. Everything matches; when you are angry you look-sound-act angry and when you are sad, you look-sound-act sad. Congruency. There are no pasty smiles or "I'm fine" when you're not. There is a match between how you feel on the inside and how you appear on the outside. It sounds so simple and yet it is so difficult attain.

I'm not suggesting we open our soul to the whole world; that would be foolish. The question is how to develop relationships with others where it is all right to be yourself. There are many levels of intimacy. For example, you would give more of your inner self to a best friend than to the store clerk you just bought groceries from. (Let's hope that is true for you.)

Congruency, like all the other *fat* words we have talked about, is not something we ever totally obtain. It is a process. We are continuously integrating all the varied parts of our selves. The next section begins to develop a frame to work from as we consider all the different parts of self and what to do with them.

Congruency vs. the Amoeba

Since birth, the brain has been gathering data and storing experiences; these are called memories. There are memories or stored information about yourself through every phase of life and every experience you have had. It's as if, stored in the brain, there is still a part of you that is an infant, a toddler, a pre-teen, a teen, and on and on. If there were a scrapbook on your lap with photos and mementos of each event in your life, each picture would represent another age, another moment. The brain is like a huge scrapbook storing all of those younger parts of self.

Listen to the language of the people around you. They constantly talk about their parts. "A part of me wants to go but another part wants to stay." Or "Part of me feels so confident but another part feels like a small child."

The words that randomly fall off of peoples' lips are not random at all. Like hieroglyphics, they are the hidden code that will tell us what the brain is doing. Language can bring us directly to the pieces of our past that may require special attention.

Trouble begins when we ignore or reject one of those parts. The unconscious uses discomfort as a signal to let us know which part requires attention. For example, when I am feeling like a small child, this is the part of me that is stored in my brain that needs my attention. Making those uncomfortable feelings the villains and treating them badly damages the relationship between the conscious and unconscious mind and incongruency is the result.

Congruency is achieved when all of our parts are aligned and working as a whole. Alignment is a great word, don't you think? It makes me think of a unified front or one of those marching bands creating marvelous formations with such precision. Ideally, a person in a state of wholeness or wellness functions like that—with all parts working together to make a beautiful formation.

The field of Transactional Analysis defined three parts: the parent, the child and the adult. This works nicely but is too general. There are literally hundreds of parts of us, each one seeking alignment with the whole. The photo album is a large one, but only the parts which are out of sync or out of step present the problems we experience in daily life.

A part gets out of sync for one of several reasons—not getting basic needs met during the younger years, too many traumatic memories, or belief systems in conflict with what a part of us desires to be or do. An example of belief systems in conflict might be one part of you loves to write, another part of you believes it is a waste of time.

Whether it is a hole in our history or belief systems in conflict, the solution is in first seeing the part of you that is calling for attention, and then finding out what he or she needs.

Far too many of us spend time wondering *why* our lives are going the way they are. Asking why will not give us the answer, only *how*—how can I make it different, create a new pattern, resolve the conflicting beliefs systems?

Getting In Sync with the Self

I believe everybody has a central core that is intact and whole. However, we are also surrounded by the many parts of ourselves and, if these parts are continually ignored and pushed back, we become like the amoeba, formless and jellylike, taking on whatever shape someone out there wants us to take on. When this happens we are out of sync and nothing goes right. We pull away from the intact core self and the personal boundary around us becomes distorted.

A personal boundary is like an invisible energy field that keeps us together just as skin keeps all of the internal organs together. We have a core or center self and all of the different parts of the self are aligned around that core. If we are pushing parts away, we begin to look more like an amoeba. We are no longer aligned around the core strong self. The ideal picture of wholeness is when our parts are in sync and aligned with one another around the core--it looks rather like ball bearings that make the wheel turn evenly. Words to describe this might be purposeful, confident, compassionate, organized, enthusiastic and charismatic.

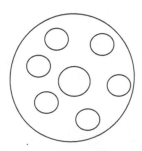

Below is a picture of a person out of sync with themselves, with their parts pushed away or scattered. Words to describe this person might include conflicted, depressed, sick, bored, aimless, victimized, unbalanced, and scattered.

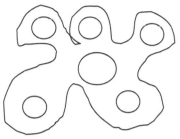

If you are wondering where the unconscious mind fits in this simple diagram, perhaps it is the space between. Its job is to get the core you working with the parts and moving toward alignment. Of course, there are all the in-between shapes—we are fluid beings, continually changing and shifting.

Total congruency is an ideal to strive for, not something we ever obtain or keep. That is what makes life interesting. As new opportunities for learning are presented we have the chance to pull the alignment even tighter. In fact, that is the process of living. As each part is pulled into alignment, we feel more integrated.

How do these different parts of the self become isolated from the core self? Again I present a case for paying attention to small signals emerging from the unconscious mind. Here Mary's internal dialogue demonstrates what can happen. Imagine the perfect circle around the core self suddenly pushing out along one edge. As the rejection of that part of the self deepens, the part pulls further away from the core.

"I hate it when my boss talks to me in that tone of voice. It makes me feel thirteen again." (Unconscious signal—the feeling.)

"Damn it. I am sick of feeling like that." (Ignoring the unconscious signal.)

As Mary continue to push the part away, the lost part gets further and further away from the center. She may begin to blame the boss (or herself) and, rather than bringing the part in closer, she gets more separated from herself.

Mary focuses on the boss instead of paying attention to the thirteen-year-old part that the boss has triggered into awareness.. Most likely, the boss isn't even aware of his tonal qualities or her response. The problem is in Mary—not the boss. If she repeats this destructive process with very many other parts, she will become amoeba-like. Mary needs to respond immediately to the primary or first feelings and act on When she does this she is gently pulling that lost part back into the center.

> "Hmmm, when my boss talks to me in that tone of voice, I feel like I am thirteen again." (Noticing the signal.)

> (Take the meta-position) "I wonder what that thirteen-year-old part of me needs?" (Assessing the need.)

> "Maybe that part of me was overly criticized and needs to be supported or defended more often." (Discovering the need.)

> "Yes. She is alright." (Tending to the need.)

When we align with the part of ourselves that is reacting, we have the opportunity to make adult and congruent choices about who we want to be and how to act. When a part of the self is tended to in this gentle and direct way, the intensity of that first feeling drains away quickly and the moment can easily be dealt with as an adult. Mary might let the boss know of her reaction to his tone of voice. If he is a considerate boss he may even change the behavior.

In the first example, the feeling of discomfort is ignored and Mary becomes angry and blaming. In the second example, she has an opportunity to grow stronger by knowing her inner self better.

Consider that the world is a mirror held up to reflect the

parts of ourselves we dislike or have abandoned. Have you ever met someone whom you instantly disliked? If we can't stand selfishness in others, we may need to consider a child-like part that is selfish or examine our old programming about selfishness. Likewise, the qualities we admire in others will be the qualities that we admire in ourselves or desire to have more of.

This is a simplified version of how the conscious and unconscious can begin to dance with each other, one leading and the other following. When we get used to being a partner to the unconscious, changing unwanted responses and patterns becomes simple to do.

Perhaps the best way to learn this process fully is to take several feelings and experiences and reframe them step-by-step so that we learn to appreciate even the highly uncomfortable feelings. Some of the feelings we commonly struggle with are anger, loneliness, fear, grief, and insecurity or inadequacy. Likewise, when we increase our ability to deal head-on with these feelings, we feel better about ourselves. Self-appreciation is generally the nice by-product or end result of learning to acknowledge and embrace each individual part of the self and what it is attempting to do for us.

Low self-worth is the end result of disliking or despising the various parts of the self and failing to acknowledge the useful intention behind the behaviors. In the final section of the book are several techniques for streamlining this process and putting it into our conscious control.

Although there are more extensive exercises in later chapters for "growing yourself up," you could begin here to identify reoccurring patterns and feelings that may be attached to the lost and younger parts of yourself. Make an early list and by staying your current age and using the overseer if needed, simply scan any memories behind the feelings you struggle with and see what comes up. An example might be something simple like a mean kid who teased you about getting glasses in third grade. I had one of those who called me "bubble eyes." It hurt her feelings and I needed to go and give her a hug.

Exercises for First Identification of Old Patterns

I feel afraid when _____.

insecure
alone
stupid
clumsy
(add a word or feeling)

The memory that comes to mind is _____.

She (he) was _____ years old when that event happened.

What she (he) needed was _____

Use this to discover any number of old patterns around insecurity, feeling stupid, feeling fat or whatever. If you are able to see the event, step back from it, and stay your age, create the feeling of stepping in and giving the younger you what she (he) may have needed. We will do more with this later.

Practice with as many of these as you want. Remember that your goal is to give attention to that younger part and to pull them back into your center core self.

Chapter Ten
Feeling Good About Bad Feelings

As several of the most common emotional experiences are presented here, be sure to plug them into your own reality and work with it there. You can begin by using the simple technique outlined at the end of the last chapter.

For each feeling, I try to show what life would be like if that uncomfortable feeling were to simply *disappear*. I offer them here only as a stepping-off place. Do scribble your thoughts in a note-book and analyze memories that emerge while you go through the list below. And do remember the foundation stones, and the languages and awareness pieces we have so carefully inspected and selected. Why become a robot? Learn to act and not simply react.

Loneliness

Isolated, apart, closed in, a desperate aching feeling in your chest and middle—you feel on the inside that nobody knows you or understands you, or even cares who you are. You feel different and all alone in your differentness. You wonder if there will ever be anyone to fill that loneliness. What will you do? Where will you go? How? When? WHO? What will ease the ache?

The truth is, you are alone, totally alone. There is no-body who can crawl into your body and see out of your eyes. You are all alone in the world. There is no right place, no right man or woman, group, church, school, commune, class or book that can remove that feeling of aloneness permanently. You walk alone.

Accept that.

And go on.

Here is how. Just for one fleeting moment, imagine having that feeling of loneliness totally removed from your being. Loneliness is gone. No twinge or twisted feeling in the middle. It is gone.

What would life be like if you had *never* experienced that

feeling? Would it be a relief? Would life be so much easier to bear? When first asked, most people think it would be wonderful for loneliness to disappear. But then ask yourself these questions:

Without that feeling, how would you know to seek like-minded people? Call a friend? Choose a life partner? Grow toward intimacy? How would you know when you needed that human warmth that only an intimate friend can give?

You wouldn't know . . .

You would have nothing to tell you this.

Loneliness is a *signal* to search out new sources of nurture. Without that awful feeling, you would truly be lonely.

Yes, if you ran the scenario worldwide and removed loneliness from the human race, there would be no need for marriage, friendship or families. Eventually, there would be no death (due to lack of population).

This may seem extreme, but how else can we come to appreciate and understand loneliness and what it actually accomplishes for us? Loneliness comes straight from our need to be loved—the two are intimately connected. Without loneliness and love, we would have no *need* for other human beings.

Can you imagine loving the loneliness? Yes, I said loving the loneliness for all it accomplishes for you, for pushing you out of your secure little nest and into a world full of surprises and possibilities. Suppose you could embrace that feeling–perhaps you even learn to ask for more loneliness, a deeper aching kind of loneliness. Several things would happen. You would:

- stop resisting the feeling,
- feel it for a shorter amount of time,
- feel it less intensely,
- develop more options for satisfying loneliness,
- have less fear of risking rejection.

Suppose loneliness is directly related to our need to be loved and nurtured. What happens when this need is not responded to, or when we have too few choices for healthy nurture? Here are few things possibilities . . .

- promiscuity,
- a lousy marriage,
- children born to fill the hole,
- extreme fear of rejection.

Fear of rejection or a deep need for approval are both faulty responses to the need to be loved and nurtured and the only flaw rests in our lack of choices on how to respond to the need. This fear spawns a host of other feelings: jealousy, possessiveness, isolation, cynicism, sarcasm, hopelessness, depression . . . .

Remember that a feeling or behavior ties directly back to one of the three basic needs—safety, love, and self-expressions.

Resolving Loneliness

A large part of our population is hungry for nurture: bars, singles clubs, even some churches or fraternal organizations are only illusions of a power source but have no power to give to you. Look long and hard for a group, or even one person who looks filled and satisfied—then seek them out—even when it scares you. Be aware that many people have the appearance of being a source but are just dry wells or will even attempt to draw power from you.

Seeking nurture is not always an easy thing to do. In the case of one client, Jerry, the loneliness had been buried for so long and his need had grown so large that he had a terrible fear of rejection. It intensified to the point that when he met a person he liked—he would reject him or her immediately to avoid the pain of the other person rejecting him. Not a good way to begin relationships and not a good way to get his needs met.

If you are too shy or afraid to reach out, then you may need to begin with a good therapist. The need is the priority here. Once you begin to take care of it, it gets easier to risk. Pay for therapy. Pay for professional massage. Do something to begin getting filled up again. However, do some homework and find out which therapist or masseuse has something to give you. Many people become therapists for the wrong reasons—holes in their history, untreated alcoholism or co-alcoholism, lack of nurture in childhood.

Find a therapist who will assist you in discovering good support groups or intimacy groups where you can practice relationships. The sooner you move into a larger human realm, the faster the needs will be filled. (Groups are often less expensive, too).

Be very cautious of being prescribed drugs that only deaden the needed signals.

It is amazing how many people stay with a therapist for a long period of time even when their intuition tells them to quit. Gary had been seeing the same therapist for almost two years with no results. I asked him why he continued to go, and he said he didn't want to be a quitter. His gut said quit, but his belief system said don't quit. This is another example of belief systems in conflict. Evidently his therapist had told him that his dissatisfaction with his progress was due to his "resistance to change." The truth was—he had a lousy therapist.

If you do feel like you are willing and able to seek the power sources around you, begin by checking out the following possible sources:

- Healthy Churches
- Healthy 12 Step Programs (AA, AlAnon, etc.)
- Intimacy Groups
- Some singles clubs (not the partying types)

You may have tried some of these options in the past without success, but keep in mind that you may be in a more open position now, actively working on the part-nership with your unconscious.

When you have linked up with a healthy source, take the time to get to know a few people intimately. Surround yourself with that energy until you can at last begin to release and let go of any former toxic friendships and connections. They cannot help you, not without work on their part.

Some people are like spiders; they build secure, sticky little webs and then invite you in. They pity you, they care for you, they keep you secure—but it becomes a deadly trap and you begin to shrink and grow smaller.

Remember, loneliness is a gift of love from your deeper self. The intention of that inner ache is only to make you expand

and enrich your life, never to harm you in any way.

You don't have to like loneliness. You just have to love and appreciate its gifts. After I have gone through several of these feelings, I will give you specific techniques for finding out which part of you (the amoeba again) is having the feelings and how to care for that particular part of you.

Fear

Heart pounding, palms sweating (or ice cold), vision distorted, armpits damp. These signs of distress are the physical symptoms of fear. Fear is perhaps one of the greatest but most misunderstood tools of the unconscious. It brings everything from mild discomfort to physical shock or unconsciousness, depending on the cause of the fear. Fear is an excellent example of how resourceful we can be; quick, strong, responsive, and incredibly imaginative, but we have lost sight of this essential response.

Fear itself is a pure response, as clean and quick as a panther's pounce. It doesn't think, it doesn't question, it doesn't play mind games. It just is.

When danger is present, fear is present. It makes us ready.

Again, keep the clean fear response separated and distant from the secondary responses you have *around and about fear.* Examples of secondary responses are loneliness, intense hatred of fear, self-criticism for feeling fear, and deep analysis on the sources of fear. All of these secondary behaviors and feelings have nothing to do with the pure fear response. They come after. They erupt out of endless belief systems, socialization, roles you *should* play, and reactions you should be having.

Shoulding on yourself, as we discovered earlier, is pro-bably the biggest killer of self-worth. If you are doing it, stop it.

Fear. What is the function, or intention it serves for our survival? Like loneliness, take a minute to imagine what your life would be like if you had never had an experience called fear. Pretend for a moment that it has ceased to exist in human experience.

When you were two years old your parents taught you to fear the busy traffic in the street, a hot stove, deep water, and fire. This teaching became so internalized that now you are automatically cautious with those things. If fear were removed, how would you know to:

85

- drive carefully on slick roads,
- lock the doors,
- protect the kids from harm,
- read labels on a medicine bottle,
- avoid vicious dogs,
- not spend the whole paycheck on a whim?

Sure, many of these things we might write off as pure common sense, but think about that phrase. Common Sense. Common Sense evolves out of small, but healthy, doses of fear over a lifetime of learning. It has become an automatic or common function of your senses.

Fear is protection. Without fear, we are an endangered species. Fear keeps us aware of danger. Fear keeps us alive.

These are actual bodily dangers at this point and emotional fears are a bit different, but I wanted to first clearly define fear.

> Fear equals safety.
> Safety equals survival.
> Survival equals life.

At the deeper level, every pure fear is given by the unconscious as a warning that life is somehow endangered and caution or action must be exercised.

It is easy to understand the intention of fight/flight reactions to danger, right? But what about emotional fear, the kind of fear that keeps us from really pursuing our goals, that stops us short and often seems vague and unexplainable? In some of the literature, I've seen it described as existential fear (whatever that means), fear of success or fear of failure.

All fear has to do with safety. Physical fear has to do with maintaining life by maintaining the physical body, and emotional fear has to do with maintaining life by maintaining the emotional or spiritual body.

The desire to live is powerful and driving. Even in the darkest times we seek a glimmer of light. It is an animal instinct to survive. The need to survive surpasses all others and sits near the top of the whole structure we call life. The question is why do we have this strong instinct to survive?

Simple. To love, to be loved . . . to create. These things are wired into the human being.

It is paradoxical. That which we need the most (to love, to create) scares us the most because, without those two items, life has no meaning.

One client, Susan, grew up in a violent and hostile environment and was bemoaning the fact that she had "wasted eighteen years of her life emotionally shut-down". I asked her to imagine herself during those hard years with her feelings wide open and receptive. Where would she be right now if she had not had the ability to shut down those feelings and close herself off from the environment?

She got real quiet and thoughtful and finally whispered, "I would be dead." Fear and a shutdown response rescued her from suicide. It was her unconscious self that provided fear and allowed her to have this protection when life became too hostile or toxic.

One silver thread that connects us all in a deep way is our need to be loved. If I begin to suspect that I may be unlovable, I become terrified and desperate. A shut-down protects me from being hurt more.

Acknowledge fear. Love fear. Welcome fear into your life. Yes, I know this is an unusual way to deal with such an intense response. Trust your fear and then choose the responses you desire instead of the lousy behaviors that spring from fear. Behaviors like:

- people pleasing,
- isolation,
- self-condemnation
- arrogance,
- martyrdom,
- jealousy,
- possessiveness,
- sick dependency,
- and on, and on, and on.

It begins to look like the spider web again. Fear is just a feeling. It is not a bad feeling! Separate pure fear from muddy responses to fear. In order to do this you need three things: your unconscious mind, a highly trained sensory awareness, and a safety net or a power source. The first two are what this book is all about, and the safety net or the power source I mentioned earlier will give you the rest. This is so important that if I overstress it, bear with me.

Note: In the years since first putting this book forth, I have discovered the inner power source of our own creative and dynamic urge. This, I believe, is as important as love. In fact, creating IS love. Dr. Lawrence LeShan, in his book, *Cancer as a Turning Point*, says that the one common element he found in his thirty years of working with cancer patients was that they had lost their "zest" for life. They no longer thought it made sense to dream, create, and envision. I've noticed in my own work with people that fashioning a dream out of the daily grind is both difficult and essential. What is your vision, your deepest hope for your life? Are you pursuing it in small, even steps—or waiting for the tooth fairy?

Resolving Fear—the Safety Net

Fear pushes us to find safe sources of nurture or a safety net. As a child, what was your safe harbor? Tony said his Chevy. Portia said her fear. Dora said her books or the woods. All of those worked, (like Susan shutting down her emotions), but a truly safe harbor has to have nurturing people in it.

A trapeze artist learning a new stunt gives himself room to learn and risk greater and greater moves by placing a secure safety net below himself to stop any falls. While you learn and mature, the world is full of hard concrete floors. A smart rock climber makes sure his rope is safely attached to the pieces of protection placed in the solid rock. It will support him in case of a fall.

Where is your safety net, your protection, the safe harbor you can pull into for repairs and shoring up when you need it? Napoleon Hill, in *Think and Grow Rich,* stresses a need for a master mind group in order to succeed in business. This is a group which supports you in a variety of different ways. They become your network, your safety net.

A quick note here—don't delude yourself into thinking there is one right knot or person who can do this for you. One knot does not make a net. Remember the loops of power that run out from you and then return to you? Be cautious of becoming overly dependent on one person whether it is a relationship or a therapist or teacher. You need people in your net-work and the nurture they give empowers you to go on.

Enough on fear. Honestly appraise and appreciate fear, discover the need that seeks protection—and become its servant. As you go through each of these feelings, notice that each of these primary needs is also our primary source of power and strength. When the needs are filled, we are free to turn our attention to greater pursuits.

As you practice working with your fears, you may notice a pattern emerging, a linkage between several of the smaller fears that indicates a theme or pattern. This theme may be one part of you that needs attention—another hole in your history to work on.

Inadequacy

The con, phony, pretend, caught—you glance over the shoulder quickly to see if anyone has noticed that you don't have the answers. Feeling inferior leads to awful feelings that make you want to lie, cover-up, cover your butt, get defensive, brag, fake it and on and on. I know you are already wondering what possible good intention all of these horrible feelings could have for you. What good can come out of all these behaviors?

Once again, take a minute to imagine your life without any of these feelings of inadequacy . . . imagine that you have never experienced this feeling. What would your life be like? How would you know when you:

- had obtained competence at a specific task,
- didn't know enough,
- needed more information,
- needed more experience,
- needed to ask questions,
- needed to strive to be better?

Sometimes we feel inadequate because we are. Would you let a person off the street perform surgery on your brain because he said he knew how and had no feelings of doubt or inadequacy? Would you contract to have a house built by a person because he said he knew how? Well, truthfully, the world is full of people who do not heed their own feelings of inadequacy and, as a result, really are incompetent. Personally, I would rather occasionally feel inadequate than *be incompetent* or negligent.

We have this crazy notion that we should know everything about every subject or we are stupid. I liked the way I heard it expressed just recently: "It is not know-how that is important . . . it is learn-how."

Feeling inadequate is a signal that puts our learn how into action. There is far too much emphasis placed on stuffing the brain with meaningless information and not enough emphasis placed on the process of being able to find any piece of information needed. It is paradoxical; the more you know, the more you know you don't know.

The great thinkers of history were great thinkers because they knew they didn't know. They could ask questions!

Of course, as with loneliness and fear, the behaviors created in response to feeling inadequate or inferior can be destructive. Lifetime habits of covering up mistakes are formed; powerful patterns of searching for a scapegoat or someone to blame are formed; huge egos are built on the shaky shoulders of the little guys. It can be a mess. And how does this happen? Because we ignore the feeling.

Risking

Risk is vital to our growth. Risking is a sign that we are flexing and stretching, reaching into new facets of the personality, and touching the outer limits of our own experiences. Risking is the sign of awakening, the beginnings of knowledge.

Think of the common American Dreams; they are powerful proof that most of our society is still asleep. Supposedly you have made it in America if you have:

- secured a paying position,
- secured a spouse or family,
- secured a pension,
- secured a home,
- secured an insurance policy.

Society feels sorry for those who have risked a large sum of money and lost, started a business and lost, left a marriage and lost. Perhaps we have no idea what those losers felt like as they stood out on the very edge of their existence and risked it all.

If you are stretching, awakening, reaching as far out as you can go—there is risk. It is an integral part of growth. In fact, it is that feeling that lets you know you are exploring new territory, sailing into uncharted waters. The word *security* is a pretend word.

We cannot *not* grow. It is a need like eating and sleeping, reproducing the species and staying warm. Much of the unhappiness in the world is caused by our dynamic urge to grow being thwarted and replaced with not so ideal ideals. Individuality and creative and risking are often abandoned for security.

Imagine a life with no risk. What would happen if children suddenly ceased taking risks? They would not climb stairs, learn to walk, explore or put their tiny arms out in a deep request for love. We are like little children all of our lives. When we at last conquer one set of stairs, our eyes spot the high table and the gears turn—how can I get on that table?

I remember watching my son, who was only one at the time, attempt to conquer a table. His desire to be on top of the table was stronger than his fear or doubt. He attempted to get up on a kitchen chair and, failing that, he pushed a box over and attempted that but he had an open end on one side and the box collapsed. Then, like a little engineer, he figured out that the box was stronger if the open end was down. Soon he was on the box, on the chair, and then on the table.

If the step is too high for you, add one. Without risk, life isn't alive. It is death.

Put it in your own context. What is your table? What do you want to climb? You may even know how to make the steps the right size, but then that logical, conscious mind kicks in and says "but you might get hurt." Over and over it has talked you out of the dream. So you stay beneath the table unable to see what marvelous, shocking articles may be waiting for you on top.

Life is a series of little miracles. The process of deciding when to risk and when not to risk is one of these miracles.

Chronic Anxiety

Chronic anxiety is a common complaint in the people I

work with. It is not possible here to define how you experience this fat word but often a gnawing anxiety or a constant sense of worry erupts from many sources. Many people worry when things are going badly, and they worry when things are going great, and they worry when things are on an even keel. Most commonly, I find that worry results from playing old tapes and movies over and over again in the mind. The intention is to keep us from repeating the negative experiences again but sometimes letting the movie and old tapes run wild causes us to recreate history.

For example, Donna's oldest daughter became preg-nant in her teen years and Donna was terrified her second daughter would repeat the error. So much worry energy went into keeping tabs on the second daughter that she nearly programmed the poor girl to get pregnant. Worry energy is wasted energy. Take the caution signal—but let the old movies and tapes stop there.

For example, if I see a bottle of bleach on the floor beside my two-year-old toddler, I could make movies of all the horrible things that could happen should he get into that bottle. The movies are good—they convince me to immediately get the bottle out of his reach. However, some parents let their movies run wild. Any awful story they hear about some child is instantly plugged into their minds as if it happened to their child. These parents often become overprotective and mothering becomes smothering.

In extreme cases, stacking anxieties can cause agora-phobia or panic attacks. It is even possible for a single event, such as a severe panic attack, to become the trigger for others. Fear of having another attack (replaying the movies and tapes) actually triggers an attack. If you are having a difficulty such as this, you may need to work with someone who can assist you in un-stacking all the feelings and behaviors that are piling in on one another from the inciting event.

Note: One new area of study that has added to my understanding of any chronic patterns of depression and fear comes from the work of Bert Hellinger and Family Constellation Work. Sometimes when we experience these chronic patterns we may be hooked (unwillingly) into the larger systemic patterns of our family of origin. This is a powerful force and bears looking into. Search the internet for Family or Systemic Constellation Work or my websites for additional information about how to release these entanglements.

Phobias/Traumas

A phobia is a bit different than other feelings or behaviors. A phobia is often attached to one or a few key events in your life. The brain imprints powerful memories, and these memories can override even your most logical thinking. For example, if you have a phobia of snakes, you may absolutely know that a snake is harmless and still not be able to rid yourself of the fear.

If you are phobic or have suffered a severe trauma: violently raped or abused, a car accident, war or a life-threatening event, you may need to seek the assistance of a trained NLP practitioner to help you change the structure of the internal movies. These traumatic events often reoccur in the form of a flashback. The intention of the unconscious is to protect you, but you may not need such dramatic protection today, and the movies can be changed. I have seen dramatic recovery from phobias and traumas using NLP interventions that work with internal movies.

And What About Sex?

Of course, I couldn't do a whole book and not at least touch on sex. Sex is not exactly a feeling. It is an experience in and of itself. Unfortunately, sex has taken the rap for too many unsatisfied needs. Sex is one of the desserts of life, one of the sweet little mints that make a whole meal taste better. How have our three primary needs gotten so entangled with sweet little sex? When it should be just the frosting, it has become the cake—or the whole meal.

Be cautious of confusing sex with intimacy. Yes, they can go together, but they are not the same. Sex has been overplayed; it seems to topple awkwardly at the top of our A-Frame structure and it doesn't belong there. It is in the bedroom that many other problems are played out, but they really have little to do with the physical joining of two people. The other problems have to do with money, love or lack of love, safety, nurture, and children or lack or children. In other words, sex sometimes becomes a catch-all for life's daily struggles.

I can imagine no lovelier thing than two evolving, aligned individuals coming together for a momentary sexual exchange. Ideally, sex is the highest physical and spiritual exchange two people can make but, in a less ideal context, it is the friction that forces people to pay attention to the other uncomfortable feelings we've been talking about here. Here the little piece of sandpaper can become a belt sander; it will either smooth the rough lumber to a fine surface or it will gouge and mar the wood. Friction—another fine tool for growth.

Just think of all the rules and belief systems that have to be sorted, and sifted, and unscrambled just to make sex a fun and nurturing experience. Sometimes, it is like wrestling alligators.

An unhappy sex life is a sure signal that you are not being fully responsive to your other needs. Things are not well with you and being that close to another human being makes it difficult to hide buried resentment, anger, and dependency. You just can't hide and have good sex at the same time.

Relating with Others

Up to this point, we have been concentrating intensely on the relationship between the conscious and unconscious mind, and developing a relationship with the self. Just for a moment, extend this knowledge to how we relate to others.

When I work with couples or groups, I often stand two people opposite each other and have them study each other for a moment. Then I place them back to back and have them take a minute to look through that scrapbook at all the younger parts of themselves: the themes, the patterns, the events they went through, the holes in their history, all of it. Then I ask them to turn around and face their partner again and recognize that all of that history can come between two people trying to relate to one another.

What sometimes appears to be the other's fault or flaw may not have anything to do with them. It may have to do with a piece of that history replaying itself. We often forget that we are looking out at the world with eyes that are filtered by our own experiential history. Although our bodies may be thirty or fifty, we are triggered back into a much younger part of ourselves or a previous experience.

For example, Rose could not understand why her preteen daughter was uncomfortable with her attempts to hug and hold her. Rose had had a severe deprivation of touching in her childhood and wanted to make sure her daughter did not suffer the same deprivation. Consequently, her daughter had had enough nurture and was ready to separate from mom in the normal teenage way. I reminded Rose that she was looking at her daughter through the eyes of her own history—not her daughter's history!

How you have mapped your experiences is totally different than how I have mapped mine—we all have our own unique map of the world.

For example, fifty people in a workshop may hear me say the word "water" and when I ask what they thought, I will get 50 unique versions of the word water. Some will see or hear a creek or a waterfall, some a lake, some a tub, some a drink. Even if all fifty people saw a creek, it could not possibly be the same creek. Like snowflakes and thumbprints, each of us is unique and we all have our own map of reality. When you and I communicate, we actually exchange maps of the world. This exchange can add to my map of the world, especially if I consider myself an explorer in new territory for the first time.

However, if I assume your map and mine are the same, we are in trouble. I begin expecting you to act in certain ways, to think like me, to dream the same dream and our relationship begins to die. How well you relate to others depends upon how willing you are to recognize another's map and how well you learn to relate to your own map.

Communicating with others can become a tennis match of exchanging histories with the ball just passing from racket to racket in a never-ending game of insult, defense, insult. This deadly game can result in lost jobs, ended marriages, and hurt children.

If the game has become destructive, there is only one way to stop it—one or the other partner must drop the racket and walk off the court. Game, set, match--it is over. No more insults. The partner still on the court may keep serving balls across the net for awhile but, before too long, he or she will realize that the game has ended. It takes two to play this game.

Once you refuse to play, you can begin searching for the need that asks your attention. Is it nature, nurture, or self-evolvement? When the need is uncovered, find ways to satisfy the need.

Beyond the three baseline needs, there are actually only behaviors and feelings left. Remember the spider web effect in our earlier diagram of the needs and behaviors?

Pick a past experience with another person where one of those damaging behaviors was displayed and take a moment to practice your new thinking about your feelings. Can you get through the tangle and see what the need was at that moment? Check it on several events. Begin to consider how the outcome may have been changed if you had responded only to the need of the moment. I know that I have said over and over again, *the behavior is not the need,* but it can make such a difference in stopping the tennis match.

The Need to Evolve

The need to continue learning is the need to self-evolve and become the best that we can be. This is the third need that sits at the top of our A-Frame.

There are many wonderful word symbols that represent this need in the language; happy, serene, successful, alive, enthusiastic, creative, peaceful, holy, but words are meaningless unless we learn to handle those feelings of inadequacy in ways that allow us to continue learning. We tend to think those lovely words are something we can own like a car or a house or a horse. They are a things—not a noun. In reality, it is the day after day, moment after moment, living habits and attitudes that need to be carefully and continuously groomed and inspected.

Being the best is a state of being. The moment you emerge from the womb (or at conception), you begin organizing life with the distinct purpose—yes purpose—of satisfying the first two pure needs—nurture and safety—so you can begin being the best. It is possible to learn to use your feelings of inadequacy to guide you toward being the best that you can be.

Can you imagine a life where feelings of inadequacy were just quick flickers to let you know where you need more knowledge or information? Can you imagine being honest enough to simply say, "I don't know" and divert all the con-job-cover-ups coming from misguided expectations about what we *should* already know? Feeling inadequate simply says, "It is important to me to gain know-how and information about this." Socrates, the ancient philosopher, gained his fame by asking questions and stating what he did not know.

Learn to make feeling inferior or inadequate a part of you that you appreciate. It is there to assist you at being the best. An overdeveloped need to "know it all" is another hole in the history that needs attention.

It is pretty difficult to think about being the best if the belly is empty and the body is cold: that is why self-evolution is at the top of the A-Frame. Satisfy the other needs first and then go to the third, although remember that there are no distinct lines between the three.

Even as I write this out I wonder, "Are there really only three needs?" I question this but every need I can think of links directly to one of these three basic needs. We need to be warm, safe, fed, loved—and we need to evolve as human beings on planet Earth. There is, however, one irritable little feeling I can't seem to find a need for.

What Do I Do With Guilt?

There is one feeling that does not seem to fit into the A-Frame of needs and behaviors, and I think it needs special consideration. That feeling is guilt.

Guilt seems to have a powerful influence on many people. What useful purpose does it have? What is its intention? It definitely is a reaction to a response--but for what reason?

I'm not referring to the kind of guilt that means, "Yes, I did do that act." That kind of guilt is self-explanatory, it is basic honesty.

But what about the free-floating kind of guilt that seems to settle in when you attempt to move out or change a lifestyle? There seems to be an overriding factor of guilt in nearly every part of our society. Women are guilty if they stay home and raise families and guilty if they choose careers. Men are guilty if they do too much around the house or if they don't do enough. It seems that if you step outside of predetermined societal boundaries, you feel guilty.

I'm confused about guilt. Does it force us at last to choose who we wish to be? Does it squeeze and pinch and wrack us with pain until we are at last forced to make a stand for ourselves, to select our own path, our own responses and behaviors?

Take the simple word "self-centered." The dictionary

defines it as, "independent of outside force or influence, self-sufficient". This is such a simple definition, and yet a whole set of rules have evolved that state that self-centeredness is bad. The meaning has been perverted and people feel guilty if they respond in ways that could be considered self-centered.

Think of your own battle with guilt. Are you truly guilty of some bad action or has this become a way to not be who you really are based on old programming? Perhaps we are not allowed to make our declaration of independence until we've completed our inner work and gained the knowledge of the self.

So how do we get rid of guilt? Just relax and know that those restraining ropes will fall away as the other work is done? Just relax and enjoy the journey, continuing to resist guilt in a way that encourages a stretch or a flexing of our own potential.

A friend once told me, "If you are feeling guilty, look around, someone is manipulating you."

If we do not grow ourselves up (the subject of this book) then we will be held in childlike constraints by our religion our boss or others. Without self-knowledge, we will continue to ask, "Did I make a mistake, am I wrong?" We will be a slave to the rules unless we question which rules can be changed or broken?

The root word meaning of the word religion means "to tie back". Do religious and social mores keep the huge human machine on-line and running smoothly as it grows socially and spiritually?

Even the nagging guilt of still not measuring up keeps the sleeper searching, uneasy, filled with a vague sense of something missing. In essence, it keeps the sleeper from going comatose or dying. And if this is all so, then guilt fits under all the baseline needs. It links them all together and keeps us moving.

Exercise

The following exercise was not a part of the original text but I include it here because my own experience says that this is a good way to create a relationship that lasts.

Clearing for Couples
Say it early, Say if often,
Say it before it becomes Impossible to say!

Most relationships crumble not under the weight of large events but under the rubble of the unspoken small things. Learning a good process for clearing the small rubble of day-to-day living prepares us to weather the larger events should they arise. Trust, intimacy, and growth flower when a space is prepared for this regular clearing of the small things.

When Milt and I got married we discovered that both of our previous marriages had crumbled under just such a weight—the small things unspoken. Because we didn't say the small things, they would all explode out destructively in an emotionally loaded moment. When we married, Milt and I agreed to accept three guidelines for our marriage:

> 1. Everything happens for a reason—
> there are no accidents.
>
> 2. There is no such thing as a "bad"
> (or unworthy) feeling.
>
> 3. And we would keep no secrets
> (of thought or action).

So, there are no accidents, no bad feelings, and no secrets. To check our progress on this Milt and I began to do a regular Clearing Session in order to create a space for information to flow in the relationship. The signal that we needed clearing is when one does not feel to the other. It's as the unspoken blows a balloon up between the two partners and rather than risk pricking the balloon and saying something wrong, both partners begin to drift away from one another. If there is no communication the balloon just gets bigger and the risk even greater. So, the solution is to clear it before it becomes too big.

The only real parameter set for a good clearing is that either partner can say anything they need to say. Often, when we are doing this, we even begin by saying "This is hard to say, but . . . ." The underlying message in this is "Be gentle with me. I am about to take a risk and I need to feel safe with you."

Be aware of any "Yeah buts" in the clearing. If you say what needs to be said and the partner automatically goes "Yeah but . . . you did or said . . . ." then you know this is straying from the purpose of the clearing session. Score-keeping and yeah buts are not allowed. The common stance in relationships is "I am unhappy and it's because of something you are doing or not doing." This leads to a dead end.

If these old, destructive measuring patterns are not allowed, then what is allowed? The secondary goal of a clearing session is not just that the stuff get dumped but that it go somewhere different and lead toward a resolution.

The clearing session gives us an opportunity to explore many of the following sometimes invisible premises for a relationship. Here are just the ones that come to mind for me.

1. What is my expectation of you? Is it a true and fair expectation?

2. What is my expectation for myself? Is it a true and realistic expectation?

3. In what ways am I making your business my business? Or vice versa.

4. Am I feeling guilty or incomplete about something and shifting blame?

5. Is what you just said somehow reflective of what I think of myself?

6. Is anybody in the family using "hostile humor." This is something I don't allow in my family (unlike the Simpsons). We do not seek intimacy or resolve issues by poking fun or making digging comments at

100

someone in the family. Everyone is allowed to be in the family without teasing, nasty humor etc., coming at them.

7. Is there a systems problem here we can recognize and redesign? For instance, if every night at supper chaos erupts right before supper, we can analyze the process   of bringing supper to the table to deter-mine if the system is messed up some-how. Perhaps the kids need a snack at 4:00 to waylay the hungries. Perhaps a crock-pot supper would save stress at suppertime. Perhaps Mom or Dad really need 15 minutes each of alone time prior to supper. Perhaps other tasks and chores are choking the suppertime traffic. All of these questions analyze the "system" instead of shouting blame and   accusations at each other. Milt and I have discovered that fully 90% of relationship difficulties are really "systems" problems. We can pick apart the system without picking apart each other.

8. Finally, what percentage of our communication difficulties relate to our systems of origin (old ways of being) and what percentage to our own inner systems? Am I staying my right age or are there things triggering me to shrink and become small again?

When we take the small problems and irritations that come up during the clearing session and look at them from the bigger picture we can perhaps begin to actually design solutions and new systems to make life go smoother.

When one of the partners says something that may be perceived as hurtful, be willing to take it in, turn it over, think of it in all of the above ways and even sleep on it for a few days before responding in kind.

A solid, trusting relationship makes it possible for us to risk new behaviors and to grow in other arenas. Taking the time and energy necessary to do these small clearing sessions can yield a big reward for both partners. Old, stale energy is released and new energy can come in. The frequency or length of the clearing sessions depends upon how often your balloon of the unspoken blows up. Initially, you may need to do it daily or weekly. Eventually, a clearing session is needed only when the drifting signal comes.

Remember, the best gift we can give to our children is to show them intimacy and trust between two parents. Children thrive when the first priority in the family is the relationship of Mom and Dad.

Note: In the original edition of this book, there were two very poorly written chapters following this one about making healthy choices and developing personal power. I could not, in good mind, subject you to those chapters so I cut them out. What I most want to say here is that our goal is to become and stay our right age and to make choices always in the direction to growth.

By paying close attention to the quickest response—usually within a half second, we truly can decode the intricate web of reaction that happens in our brains and learn to act instead. I will replace the missing chapters with a more specific technique for growing ourselves up. The later techniques I'll leave alone.

Chapter 11
Techniques for Growing Ourselves Up

Now it is time to employ specific techniques for fine-tuning your ability to respond to the unconscious. The quickest way to accomplish this goal is to stop right here, go get a pen and a notebook, and get ready to do some writing. Many people resist writing. They are afraid to see exactly who they are by putting the words to paper, and they are afraid of others seeing who they are, but writing is the easiest way to chase unconscious material out of the depths unless you are extremely good at meditation or self-hypnosis.

Much of this book has been spent observing large, vague patterns from a distance. Now we will reverse that position and begin specifically defining which behaviors and feelings are acting out in your signal system right now.

Scan over the past few weeks in your mind. On a piece of paper, write out any behaviors experienced, or feelings you have had, that you would normally call negative or non-useful; experiences that you feel are getting in your way and keeping you from achieving your goals. Give them any word-label that you choose as long as you can recall the full experience by the word you select. Just for now concentrate on feelings attached to single events (not broad, overriding experiences like bing "bored with life"). Write down and number these events. Beside each event, write down a personality trait that you would attach to the set of feelings you had. Example: Felt inferior and inadequate with my boss/low self-worth or felt nine years old with my spouse/immature.

There is a good chance that several of these feelings are very familiar to you; this indicates that they are a theme or a pattern in your life. The desired outcome with the following techniques is to discover the unconscious signals hiding in the behaviors presented. Remember that the main goal is to find out which need is presenting itself; what is that feeling or behavior trying to do *for* you?

Also keep in mind that you are going for the unconscious

responses. If you are not used to listening for that inner response, you may want to second guess or tell yourself, "Ah, this is stupid. My unconscious is not talking to me." When I first began using all of these techniques in my journal, it took quite a while for me to begin to trust that unconscious information . . .back to developing that teamwork again. Give it time. Use the techniques and practice and let your unconscious know you are willing to work with it. These techniques are not another set of rules but an organic exploration of the symbols and metaphors offered by your deeper self. Do not force it—let it flow.

Technique #1
Parenting a Younger You

The brain is a wily character. Its sole mission is to protect you from future humiliation and pain. It has captured all of your life experiences into the complex neural network at the top of your skull. The brain is rather stupid, really. It has no real sense of time and place. Experiences captured many years ago can be triggered as if they were here and now. That teasing you got in kindergarten, that jilting you got in seventh grade, that bad speech you made in sixth grade—all are still stored there in the network.

The brain is ever vigilant, your protector, your champion and the slightest trigger from the outside world will send you time traveling, zinging back to that awful moment. In a split second you can go from being a fairly competent adult with many resources—to a powerless child once again. A single tone of voice, a smell, the sound of a bus going by, a door closing—anything can act as a trigger. Most people recognize this as so. However, most people don't know what to do to restore their right age instantly again. The more painful or dangerous or powerful the past event—the more complete the time shift.

When we are children, our lives revolve around doing the right things to please the adults around us. We don't want to screw it up and risk losing love or attention or worse. As adults, however, we need to take the occasional risk in order to design the life we most desire. In fact, the experiences of childhood often shape us as adults and this can be sometimes positive—and sometimes negative.

In a recent training I attended for mentoring children of incarcerated parents, the presenter offered a simple formula. Denise Johnston said that human development can be expressed this way—developmental insults plus developmental supports equals developmental outcomes. In other words, who you are today is the result of the number of insults you experienced plus the supports you had around you. The good news is that even if your insults outweigh your supports, this can still be changed.

A developmental insult can be anything from the terrible early loss of a parent, to a teacher who made you feel stupid or a mean kid who made you feel ugly. I remember in third grade when I went to school in my new glasses for the first time, a little boy called me "bubble eyes." For years after I felt ugly in glasses—from a single, heartless comment.

A developmental support can be a kind neighbor, good parents, a savvy teacher, good friends or, as in the technique presented below, your own self. As we progress through these steps, I'll offer more ideas on what to gather around your self for additional positive support. Remember the equation; insults plus supports equals outcomes.

Think about what happens when you consider making standing up for yourself with a boss or coworker, or making a presentation to a large group. As soon as the feelings begin to come up, notice them, and then notice any thoughts, images, memories that come up with those feelings. This is a critical step. If nothing clear comes to mind, then ask your self, "How old am I when I have these feelings?" Take the first age that comes to mind. It is usually the right one even if no specific memory comes to mind.

The first step to healing these old neural quirks is to seek and find the source of the inciting incident. You want to identify it, but you want to keep yourself from time traveling to that ancient history. Stay your right age while you seek. My experience in working with many people with phobias or painful memories is that the inciting incident will come quickly to mind. There may even be several memories clustered around a single feeling. This is normal. I think of it as a seed incident which grew into a cluster.

So here are the simple steps to correct the neural programming. I'll list each step individually and then go through the process with a few examples so you can follow along.

1. Repeat your current (real) age aloud.
2. Allow the image of that younger you to come to mind. Identify his or her age.

3. Review the event making sure you see the little one as distinct and apart from who you are currently. Sometimes placing the picture in a small still-life, contained within a frame ten or twenty feet away from you will aid you in making the separation. More on this later.

4. Ask yourself, what would I do if that were my child, niece, nephew or a nice neighborhood kid? What kind of comfort, support or intervention do they need? Come up with several possibilities.

5. Remake the scene as if you were directing a movie and this time place your adult self as a kind auntie or uncle or friend to the little child and implement one of the alternative possibilities.

6. Stay with the scene until you see the child become free, and happy again. Imagine buying him or her an ice cream or go to the park. You are reprogramming your brain—it takes a few minutes.

Now these steps seem simple but you will be surprised how difficult it is to stay your right age long enough to complete the movie remake. Most of us habitually time travel. To bring this into consciousness takes practice. When I'm working with serious trauma such as sexual abuse or a car accident, I often have to hold the person's arm and remind them again and again of their current age in order to complete the movie remake in an effective way. Once you slide into the old scene, you are lost for a moment. Essentially, you become the child again and lose your resourceful, adult self.

There are several helpful things we can do to keep the time/space separation going while we do the remake. One is to imagine your self sitting in the balcony of a grand theater watching the old scene on a screen down below. If it is a very painful event, shrink the screen to the size of a postage stamp and set it apart from you—as far as you need to in order to reduce the emotional impact. The smaller you make it, the less impact it has. And always be sure you can see the younger self in the picture. If it is still too overpowering, freeze all action and make it a still life image. Distance, color, motion, sound— all these things are the texture, the submodalities of your stored memories. We can manage and manipulate them until they lose their power.

If you have trouble holding the time/space separation between you (the adult), and you (the child), spend a moment strengthening the current, real you or practice on less painful memories. Audibly remind yourself of all the things you have accomplished as an adult. "I am a college graduate, a grandmother; I live a beautiful life and am successful at my work."

Here is another way to consider the difference between the adult you and the child you. Think of it like two cups. The cup the child is holding is very small. He or she doesn't have many resources and often feels helpless and alone. The cup you (the adult) are holding is larger and fuller. You've spent ten or twenty or thirty years filling this cup with knowledge and insight, and you have done so very consciously. You have far more resources than the child does and you must pour what you have in your cup into the child's.

Here is an example. A woman, I'll call her Kathy, was the poor kid in the neighborhood. Her clothes were homemade, her shoes scuffed, and her hair never quite neat and combed. Her daddy drank too much and mom had to work extra hard to make ends meet. The kids at school teased her, and this drove Kathy inward. She liked books and was a good student, but she couldn't participate in school activities with ease. When she was in third grade, her mother divorced her father and moved to a new town. Now she had to enter a new classroom full of strangers and the teacher was not nice. The first day, she tried to wear her very, very, very best dress but when she walked into the school, somebody called her "Raggedy Ann".

All of the above would be lumped together as "developmental insults".

Kathy endured, but uneasily. Because of this rocky beginning, she learned to pay attention to what people need and is sensitive, educated, and kind. She has surrounded herself with good friends and a nice husband. When she started writing, she joined a few critique groups, took some classes, and studied her craft with careful attention. All of these are developmental supports.

Today, Kathy is a brilliant writer, thirty-five years old. She has been lonely but has managed fine as long as she had her books and her nice, quiet husband. Suddenly, Kathy shyly enters the Pen-Hemmingway Award, wins, and is shot into the spotlight. People want to know who she is. People want to meet her. The third-grade Kathy panics. She considers turning the award down, leaving town, never writing another word.

Kathy comes to see me, (an accomplished time traveler) and learns that she, in fact, is *not that third-grade girl any longer*. Rather, she has worked very hard to get where she is and has many resources.

We sit together and I put a nice gray stone in her hand. It has some weight. It has texture. It is a beautiful stone. I have her remind herself of all that she has done, her careful study of craft, her first publication, her marriage, the brave birth of her three children, the time she told her boss off and walked out—anything we can find that she is proud of. I have her place all of those things into the stone and then hold it as if her life depended upon it for, in fact, it does. Now we time travel with intention.

Kathy sits in the high balcony in the theater of her mind, the weight of her many resources in her hand, as we look back through almost thirty years of time to the shy, silent, lonely girl in third grade. On the distant screen, we see the girl sitting alone, see her walking to school with a tummy ache, see the bully meet her at the door of her new school.

Once or twice Kathy tumbles through time and becomes the unhappy little girl again, but I'm watchful and catch her tumble. I remind her of her right age, remind her that the child is lucky because the adult Kathy is nearby and can intervene. When the separation is firm and complete, I then instruct Kathy to feel, see, smell, taste, and hear her adult self go down the sidewalk to that young girl's side.

Usually, at this point, the person I'm working with knows exactly what to do to make things better for the child. Comfort her, hold her, walk with her or whisper to her that the bully is just a bully who doesn't know his nose from a hole in the ground.

You'll be amazed how little it takes to correct the neural pathway in the direction of feeling good again. Moments only and the girl or boy lost inside suddenly feels sheltered and protected. When I'm working with an individual, I can usually see the moment when the old insult is repaired. There is usually a profound look of relief, a bit of grief, and a smoothing out of all the old fear and sorrow. It is a beautiful moment, one I've been privileged to share hundreds of times.

Don't ask me to offer you the science of this. I can't. I've studied the brain extensively and find no other reason for this time-traveling brain to be unruly except that it is trying to protect you from further harm. Once you take over the job, it is done.

Paradoxically, you'll discover that we often get so angry with those shy, unhappy parts that we end up doing to ourselves what was done initially. We call ourselves names or push ourselves into painful situations which trigger the initial response. If we take the corrective measures and we do it gently and with great compassion, the mind heals itself.

It works. I've helped clients recover from severe trauma, overcome phobias, correct storage of an unhappy childhood and, basically, become their own developmental supports to overcome the insults. There is no need for therapy and no ongoing struggle.

If you have had many insults to your childhood development, the best thing is to practice first on relatively minor incidents and work your way up to the harder ones. The key to success with this technique is to stay your right age. Only in your full adult self will you have what the little you needs or wants. And you will know exactly what that is because you lived through it.

If you have trouble staying your right age while you remake the scene, it is sometimes useful to place your own strong mentors or even spiritual guides on either side of you or a kind grandmother behind you to support you while you remake the scene. This can help maintain the separation and add strength so we can stay present.

A final thought about this. When you are playing with this technique, don't try to intervene with whoever is causing the problem—the bully or the teacher or the nun or the parent. Just focus on the child. I suggest no violence. We don't want to ever introduce violence as a solution. If the situation is extreme, as in abuse, rape or severe trauma, just whisk the child away from the situation and take them to a safe place. With severe trauma victims, we often spend time choosing that safe and beautiful place before we attempt a "rescue."

The very best is when you become your own therapist and mentor. It took me awhile to realize I could counsel or comfort the 'me' from last year. It isn't just for children. I can remake any movie scene that causes me discomfort.

A few years ago there was what some called "the inner child" movement, where therapists and writers taught people how to nourish and play with the inner child. There are some distinct differences between that movement and what I present here. While the playfulness and creativity of childhood is something we all should maintain elements of, we don't want to *become* that child again. Our goals are, or should be, very adult goals now.

We want forward motion, a strengthening of self and the supports around us. We want a strong voice. We want to be proactive in life and not acted upon. In truth, too many of us are running around the world in big bodies with a childlike approach to life. Only a strong adult can take on the challenges we face. We want to learn to notice and support that inner child (or children), but take our place as adults in the world. This technique works to do that.

I worked with a forty-four year old woman once who had had a very difficult life. She was sexually abused by a trusted family member at seven years old and had never made it into her forty-four year old body for any extended length of time. When I anchored her adult state and we together confronted the abuser and took the girl away with us, her life began to shift completely. She now repeats her mantra, "I'm a forty-four year old woman with many strengths and resources" daily and begins to believe it. You can see it on her face, in the way she walks, and in the way she holds her head. She has at last left the seven-year-old behind by taking her with her.

Because this first step is such an important one to overcoming old developmental insults, I'll give you another full example from my own life. A story goes along with it.

In the early eighties when I first began trying to "grow myself up" with this method, I went to a friend's house one night for supper. Diane was excited and elated because her daughter had just gotten her first period. She'd bought her girl a beautiful present and was planning a nice dinner celebration.

I was brought up in a strict Catholic home where we simply didn't (couldn't?) talk about such matters in public and just being with Diane made all kinds of uncomfortable things rise up in me. Later that night, I was driving home somewhat stunned by the emotions this had triggered within me. When I got home I sat down in a chair and asked myself, "How old am I?" Images rose up from far back in my memory, of a young shy fifth grader (yes, the flute player) getting breasts, getting teased, no help from mom, of mean boys snapping bra straps, of a sadistic gym teacher who made menstruating girls go to study hall instead of swimming and that study hall where cruel boys knew exactly why you were there.

It was quite a collection of memories relating to accepting my female development, my blossoming young self. It was painful. I had to force myself to sit in that chair and review each memory as it came up. I had to stay my right age. In this instance, because there were so many of those young, shy girls, I decided to try a group approach. I made a movie of my adult womanly self walking down a forested, country road. The shadows in the trees we thick and the branches hung down over the road. I (my adult self) was on the road alone but I sensed the shy girls were off in the woods, not far away but too scared to come out. I called to them, told them they were safe now and nobody would make fun of them again. I would care for them from now on.

It was so beautiful to see these blonde, awkward, beautiful young girls attached to all of my painful memories about becoming a woman emerging from the shadowy forest. One by one, I comforted them and asked them to walk with me now, that I would be in charge of their care. By the time I finished that walk down a wooded road, I must have had a dozen young

111

girls with me—and there were big tears of relief rolling down my very adult cheeks.

Some deep wound was now covered, stitched together, and corrected. Again, I can't exactly explain why this works, but I do know that it *does* work. Put it to the test. Bring those shy, blushing selves forward and take gentle care of them.

For those of you who insist on a theory of why this works, I explain it this way. All old emotional and behavioral patterns consist of neurons firing away in the brain at lightning speed. They form patterns rather like a scratch in an old record will follow the scratch rather than the grooves. These grooves are old triggers, old firing patterns, leading to old behavior. In order to make a change, we need to *burn* a new neurological pattern. Instead of going small like a child, we add a step where the older self steps in to help. With practice and constant interruption of the old pattern, the new can take hold and take over.

To learn more about this time traveling phenomena, watch both your own patterns and other people. You will improve your ability to recognize the altered state of the time traveler. Watch people in stores, restaurants or social events. Watch their faces and demeanor, the triggers that are setting them off constantly, and see if you can identify when another person shifts from their current age to one much, much younger. You can get pretty good at this. The child-like qualities take over. I've had clients twiddle their hair, bite their nails, and swing their feet like a child. Usually it's more subtle, but you can train yourself to see the time shifts.

In fact, eventually you'll begin to identify individuals who have never been their right age—not for a moment. They are perpetual children, little boys and girls in big bodies. Their development was halted somewhere along the way and they've failed to thrive. Unfortunately, sometimes we discover ourselves married to such a person, or working for such a person, and life can be challenging. Their patterns kick off our patterns and the workplace or the home becomes a playground full of children.

As you get more adept with this practice, don't limit its use to correct any negative patterns. Notice the moment you or your spouse/partner lose your adult ages and become whining, sparring children. Ask continually, "How old am I? How old is he/she?" The results of this level of observation may surprise you. Studying people this way will also add to your observational skills.

Before I go on to the next step, let me explain that fixing yourself firmly in your right, adult age will free up a tremendous amount of time and energy previously spent in switching time and space. Use this released energy to become a better observer. Watch others. Listen. If you are in a dull meeting, watch the faces of others and see if you can notice the moment the speaker loses the audience's interest, when they become bored or restless.

A final thought. Once you have resolved the little girl, little boy fears, you will also want to begin consciously deciding which qualities or characteristics you admire in others and how to put those habits, skills, etc., into your own body. It's called modeling. All children learn by modeling and, likewise, all adults learn by modeling. Choose good mentors and models for whatever you hope to achieve. Identify in small details in how your model acts, speaks, and behaves. A great deal of research has been done that indicates that mental practice of the skills and qualities you hope to embrace will greatly improve your ability to carry them off.

The world is full of good models or good practices we can use (steal?) to continue to build confidence and ability. Make use of them.

The Guided Dialogue Technique

Imagine you are a scriptwriter and are preparing to write out a script between two conflicting characters in a play. They are basically squaring off to have it out and resolve the conflict. By becoming the writer of the script, you automatically take the meta-position or overseer role we talked about earlier which will give you a clearer view of the whole scene. Here are the steps to follow in writing the script. You may want to preview the steps before beginning so you can just follow the script. Select one of the uncomfortable experiences you listed earlier or choose another that you would like to have a different outcome for.

Step One: Name the two characters involved. Usually the first character will be you, the conscious mind. Go ahead and give that character a name. Now choose an event.

Step Two: Now select one of the labels (inadequate, stubborn, procrastinator, defiant, angry, scared) and define this as your second character. You know the feeling that goes with the label, so build the character from this information. Ask yourself what age this second character is, how does he or she look, what qualities, facial expressions, voice qualities. This part of you can even be represented by someone you know (a parent, spouse, child) and then name it. Example: the character is called Inadequate Part. This part of me feels like she is 13 years old, she is kind of tall and thin and early adolescent and blushes a lot.

Step Three: Begin the script by writing a few lines on the scene or the event that was attached to the feeling. The purpose of this part is simply to set the scene and recall the feelings that went with it. Write whatever comes to mind as a scene.

Step Four: You now have characters and the scene set. The feelings between the two characters represent the plot or conflict. Remember you are writing a script so you will include any words, feelings, actions or

114

images that you feel inspired to write. Good. Roll the scene. Begin by having the part that is you confront the second character with how you feel about the behaviors being displayed. This is the only place in the script where you get to unload feelings about the feeling. Call that part out and name the game and exactly how you feel about it. Address it directly. Example:

ME: Listen you inadequate little thirteen-year-old. I have had it with your antics. How dare you make me feel like such an immature fool at work . . .
(See complete sample script at the end of this technique.)

Step Four: After you have called out the conflicting character and had the first character tell them exactly how he or she feels, move directly into discovering the intention of that behavior. Demand that the conflicting character let you know what its intention is and then wait for the character's response. Remember that the intention is always a plus, not a minus.

Note: It is crucial at this point in writing the script that you quickly write the response of the conflicting character without questioning its validity. Use the first response that you get whether it is an image, a feeling, or words. Stay with it until you get a response. That character is not used to being directly confronted so you must reassure it that you mean business and will not let go until you discover the intention. If you have had many years of refusing to respond to the unconscious, it will take a bit to get some trust going. I have even used this with clients who had a suicidal part and we were able to find the positive intention of that part. The intention always leads to those basic needs again. Dismiss nothing that comes to you. If you fail to respond, or dismiss the information as stupid or silly, you will continue to be in conflict; stuck in those familiar patterns. So, notice resistance, acknowledge resistance and affirm your commitment and then move past the resistance with insistence.

Resistance is the very point of discovery of new Knowledge.

That is how you know you are very close to the heart of the pattern. The goal here is for you to obtain new information and new choices around a familiar and uncomfortable old pattern. Old patterns may have worked in the past when you were younger and had fewer resources, but they need to be cleaned up occasionally as you grow.

Step Five: When you have uncovered the intention, then get a dialogue going between the two characters that brainstorms several choices on how to satisfy the intention, or the deeper need, with new and more satisfying behaviors. Stay with it until you have at least five new choices. You may even need to introduce a new character at this point, a creative part, or a problem-solving part.

Step Six: After your characters have come up with the five new behaviors, ask if there are any other characters that have a problem with these new behaviors. If any emerge, address their objections and discover choices around satisfying them.

As you do this guided dialogue, remember that you are actually dipping into the unconscious mind for answers. You are acknowledging the partnership between you and your unconscious. Also, you may notice a few things when first beginning this process. First of all, the character you bring into your script may not have much faith in your commitment and may initially resist. If you notice this refusal to respond, just continue to affirm your need to know the intention so that you can begin responding to it and making sure all of the parts of you are unified and aligned. Don't worry if you feel silly or contrived. Society often looks at people who hear words inside or see images, as crazy or off the wall. I'm often amazed at how uncomfortable a client can get with admitting that he or she hears "voices". The truth is, everybody sees and hears this on the inside. It is called thinking.

Below is an actual dialogue done by a client using this technique. The result was a reduced fear of public speaking. The part of her that she needed to address was a "scared little girl" part. I include it here as a sample and have annotated my thoughts in parenthesis.

M: Listen little girl, I have had enough of your tortured look and trembling fear. You have to stop this nonsense. (Call the part out)

LG: I don't know what you are talking about. I don't do anything. (resistance)

M: I know. That is what I mean. You hang around my neck like a crushed and broken butterfly on a chain. God, I hate you and I hate how you make me feel! (Unload the negative feelings)

LG: How can you say that? I never asked to be hung around your neck. Do you think the heavy chain is easy to bear? I can't even heal myself in these chains. It is killing me.

M: Well, who the hell chained you there, and why?

LG: I don't know. (crying)

M: Stop it. You make me sick when you are such a little baby.

LG: See. I can't even get out of the way of your awful verbal abuse. How is it that you think I have never healed these poor broken wings? I cannot do it alone.

M: Come on...who put the chain there in the first place? What is your intention for me? (Ask for intention)

LG: It has been here so long, I have no idea how it was put there, and by whom.

M: Can't we just unhook it? What sort of chain is it?

LG: It is well woven, and continuous. The only loose link is the one connected to me . . . here by your heart.

M: It strains my neck to even try to see the connection. It hurts to try to see.

LG: Please try. Don't quit. I am so weakened by this link. I can't heal.

M: Why should that matter to me? I don't even want to see you.

LG: But you said wearing me around your neck was weakening you also.

M: Yes. You are between me and everything I want for myself. I want to know what you are trying to do for me.

LG: Please. Look then. Try to see the connection.

M: Why the hell are you so concerned? It seems to me that you have the easy end of this . . . the free ride.

117

LG: You are so dense. Don't you understand that I am you also? We are not separate. You cannot leave me behind.

M: But you are so disgusting and immature.

LG: That is the point. I am only so because you refuse to look at me. Now look for the link. What do you see?

M: I see a broken butterfly on an endless chain.

LG: Yes, but the link? What is the link?

M: All right. It is a small circle with a tiny opening where the two ends meet.

LG: But what is the link hooked to?

M: I . . . I can't see it.

LG: Please look.

M: I will try. I see your small wormy body, your weak wings cracked and trembling still. I just can't see the connection . . . wait . . . oh God. There is none. You are loose, only laying beside the tiny link. How could you do this? How could you stay there all of these years and not get out of my way. You were not linked in . . . just a free floating piece of my past laying there. What is the matter with you?

LG: Oh no. All of these years you told me I was hooked to you. I couldn't see it for myself. My eyes are too little. I needed you to see it from your bigger eyes. I only wanted us to not look foolish or be laughed at. I didn't know I was not linked into who you are now.

M: If this weren't so damn sad, I would laugh. What now little butterfly? Where will you go now?

LG: I guess I need some time to mend my wings. Mind if I just "hang around" for a while?

M: Funny! Try to stay with me and lot be in my way?

LG: That is really all I ever wanted. I am your child, the little you from back there. There is one thing I need from you though.

M: Sure... what is that?

LG: No more name calling when things get rough. I can't handle the abuse. Just pay attention to me once in a while and I won't be so hard to have around. (The true intention)

M: I can't promise . . . old habits are hard to break, but I will try to remember. Just flutter a bit to remind me when I am ignoring you.

LG: Thanks.

As you can see, it often happens that the "problem part" is a younger part of us that has been ignored or abused. The intention? Take care of her. Treat her kindly and gently. If there is a hole in your history, fill it in by parenting the child the way she originally needed to be parented—with love.

Technique Two: The Committee Meeting

Like the script writing, this technique can either be written or done with visualization during a quiet moment. Its purpose is the same as the script—to uncover the hidden intention behind an unwanted behavior pattern. Begin, as before, by identifying the behavior or the label for the experience that you want to change. This is the agenda for your "committee meeting."

Step One: Call in the committee members that you feel may have input into this meeting. Some members may include you, (the conscious mind), the problem behavior part, the creative part, the mediator part, a parent part, or whatever members you feel need to be present. Imagine them all around a circular conference table.

Step Two: Call the meeting to order and state the agenda and why it is has been brought to the attention of this committee. State the desired outcome of the meeting.

Step Three: Generate discussion about the possible intention of the presenting behavior (the part responsible for the problem).

Step Four: Discover the intention and generate choices from all members of the committee around how to satisfy the intention in new ways. Seek agreement by all members of the committee, especially the identified behavior. When several new choices have been generated and accepted, the meeting is over.

A quick synopsis of one client's meeting went like this. The problem part was a "Nag." It nagged at her constantly about all the things she should or shouldn't be doing and judged her mercilessly. The "members" she called together were herself (the conscious part), The Nag, a mediator, and her creative part. The Nag was asked point blank what her intention was in nagging and criticizing constantly. After much discussion, the intention came out this way. The woman would not listen to a gentler persuasion. After constant nagging, she would finally get mad enough to take action and/or speak her heart. All of the choices generated had to do with being more receptive and willing to speak her heart sooner—without the nagging.

Another client who suffered from chronic headaches had a similar committee meeting and discovered that the onset of a headache coincided with times she was not "speaking her heart". As she learned to respond quickly, the headaches subsided.

You will notice as you practice several of these techniques that you will begin to get clean answers faster and faster. All of these parts of you really do just want to learn to work together as a team. Rejecting parts of the self is the main cause of disintegration and problems.

Technique Three: Stream of Consciousness

This method provides your unconscious with the opportunity to free-associate without conscious interference. It is very important for you to let the pen do it for you and not think about what you are writing.

> Step One: Give the experience a name (from your list) and write the name several times and then begin writing whatever comes to mind. This method lacks the discipline of the previous two but has the same guidelines. Trust whatever comes to mind and let the pen take you directly to the heart of the behavior and its intention for you.

> Step Two: Continue until you have new understanding about that behavior. Again you can expect to hit a point of resistance. When it comes, remember that this is the strongest move toward understanding and keep that pen moving no matter what. If you stall out, just keep writing the last word you wrote until the flow returns. Here is an example.

Fearful part. Running scared, trying to get away, from what? Hide. Run and hide, run and hide. Hiding, hiding, hiding, hiding, safe, invisible, don't notice me, don't criticize me, don't blast me, fear of blasting, fear of hiding, fear of criticism, from who? from what, what, what,? me? Them? what's wrong? Who is criticizing? Me. Me, me, me... Of course. Be gentle, Be kind. Be safe. Come out.

Variation: It is interesting to try this technique with physical pain. Physical pain is often a metaphor for emotional pain and in addressing it this way, you can discover that the physical pain is about. Here is an example.

Back pain . . . pain in the back . . .pressure . . . heavy dull thud in the lower back. Pain in the back? What in my life is a pain in the back . . .get back . . . held back . . . backing up . . . from what? From self? From success. Holding back what? Holding back me? How, holding back?

It is even possible to get immediate relief when the source of the pain is uncovered using this technique, and choices are made to relieve the pressure of the moment

Technique Four: The Story

Think about the pattern you want to change. In this technique, you must decide prior to writing the story what you want the outcome to be. Take a past event and replay in your mind how you would have liked it to end, and then write out the entire scene with dialogue but change the course and the ending of the exchange to what you want it to be. For example, take a hurtful argument you may have had with a loved one. What outcome would you rather have had in that particular event?

Now, imagine the new outcome fully as you write it out. Note every difference; how would you have sounded? Looked? What would you have said? Notice as you write out the ideal whether any other feelings come up that may be keeping you from responding in this way. There may be other patterns here that need their own technique.

This technique works very effectively in meditation by just pretending you are watching and remaking a movie in your mind of the event. As you remake the scene, make sure that you are there watching and listening with your own eyes and ears (associated as opposed to dissociated). Once you gain some experience with changing your movies, you will begin to change entire patterns of behavior. The brain does not care if the movie was "real" or "pretend". It accepts the change.

Technique Five: Mental Rehearsal

This technique is very similar to the last but is especially effective when there are new behaviors that you would like to create or improve on. This technique has been used often by professional athletes, musicians and dancers to improve their style. It has four basic steps.

Step One: Select a behavior that you have seen in another person that you would like to have for yourself. Make a full movie in your mind of that person in action. Create as much detail as you can, noticing all the qualities . . .every move . . . every tone . . . whatever it is that you like.

Step Two: Now, using the same movie, superimpose your image over the person that you chose. See yourself having those exact same qualities. Improve on them if you would like. It is good to make adjustments unique to you. When you have seen yourself in the entire movie, move on to step three.

Step Three: Have the sensation of stepping into the movie and becoming a part of it. Hear what you would hear, see what you would see, feel what you would feel. Now play the entire movie YOURSELF go through all of the motions one by one in your mind.

Step Four: Now imagine several times in the near future where you would like to see those new behaviors displayed. Again make a movie of each time feeling yourself make all of the new adjustments in that scene. The more times you practice, the better it will be.

Technique Six: The Reunion

This technique is especially effective when the behavior is tied to a piece of personal history. You can usually recognize it when the feelings remind you of being a younger you, perhaps a teen or a toddler. It so often happens that we end up treating the younger parts of ourselves exactly the way they were treated initially—the treatment that began the non-useful pattern.

For example, if you were an awkward child and were teased because of that, you may strongly dislike any behavior that seems awkward to you as an adult. If you are being hard on yourself at these times, you may be treating that younger part badly and continuing the pattern.

> Step One: When a feeling comes up that reminds you of being a child again, take a moment to recall a full image of yourself at that age. Use a photograph if necessary. Imagine that child part there in the room with you.

> Step Two: Chances are that you dislike the part of you that acts that way and are making that little child part feel unloved. Imagine sitting the child on your lap or next to you on a sofa and asking it in a gentle tone of voice what it needs from you. This is the point again where that part may not trust you or may resist. Just keep insisting that you need to know how you can help him or her. Usually the child just wants love and protection and you can reassure them that you are willing to do this. In order for this to be effective, you must fully imagine that child asking for your love and support. Use a doll or stuffed animal if you need to.

> Step Three: Once you have fully reassured the child inside, promise that child that you will make a better effort to be less critical and more caring and that you will not allow anyone else to treat her badly either. Again, this has to do with strengthening that partnership and aligning all the parts of us. Like any child, they need consistency in order to feel loved and secure.

I've seen this simple technique make major transformations in a person's life. The hole in the history is quickly repaired when the time is taken to heal it. One suggestion, however; if the event was an especially painful moment in your history, you may find it difficult to keep yourself from flashing back as if it were happening again. One effective way to handle this is to put the event with the younger you in a very small frame and far from you initially. It is tough to keep out of the movie if it is a painful memory. Sometimes assistance from a trained practitioner is necessary. Unfortunately, it is sometimes difficult to find a therapist with NLP training. Keep looking. It is highly effective.

Technique Seven: Creating a Safe Harbor

It is often difficult to make quick decisions in the hustle and bustle of daily life. This technique helps you create a special place that you can go to consult other parts of yourself when a decision is pending. Once established, the place is in your own mind and is always available to you.

> Step One: Take a few moments to relax and do some deep breathing. Clear out the clutter of the moment and feel yourself unwind. Now, in your mind, create an image or idea of a place that would be uniquely yours. It may be an office, a nice little cabin in the woods, a laboratory—whatever seems right for you. Make this special place everything you would like it to be and that it is just for you and cannot be invaded by outsiders.

> Step Two: When the design is complete, place yourself in that special room and feel how secure and safe you are in there knowing that nothing can enter that space unless you invite it in. When you begin to feel at home, you are ready to invite your guide in to assist you.

> Step Three: Your guide may be a person you already know, a person from history, or even be a future you, perhaps ten years from now. Usually the unconscious will provide you with the perfect guide that will help you get what you want from life. You'll find that your guide is always in that special place ready to assist you in making decisions. Practice going there every night before you go to sleep to consult or check in with the guide. You need not let anybody else enter this part of your world. It is for you only.

Technique Eight: The Letter

This is a simple journaling letter that is especially effective when you are troubled with your relationship with another person and feel confused about the feelings. Sit down alone and take out a sheet of paper and write that person a letter. Tell the conscious mind to take a walk and then allow the unconscious mind to let you know exactly how you are feeling about that person and your relationship with them. This letter is just for you. You do not need to mail it.

At the end of the letter, spend some time telling that person exactly how you wish to be treated, talked to, related with. Affirm that you do deserve to be treated this way. You may even want to try the Mental Rehearsal Technique to practice letting that person know how you feel. I have had the unusual experience of writing this letter and then having that person begin treating me the way I desire with not a single word from me. Remember, we teach others how to treat us.

Technique Nine: The Parable

Jesus taught with parables, little stories that carried a larger message. When you feel confused or lost, try writing a parable. Create a student (you) and a teacher (greater wisdom) and then let the story unfold naturally. The student wants to learn, the master wants to teach.

Let your deeper self direct the story from within. Below is an example of a parable that I wrote for my own guidance. The story is from a series about an old sculptor named Miguel and his apprentice Joseph.

Raking Apples

For nearly a year Joseph had followed Miguel's instruction, working steadily and watching his skill as a sculptor improve. It was fall again and the air outside the studio quickened with the near onset of winter.

"How do I know I have talent, Miguel? How can I tell?"

"Perhaps, Joseph, you must learn to trust your talent and yourself. It is a gift that has been given to you. How is it that you doubt?"

"Trust! This is a wonderful word, but what does it mean? How do I get it? Tell me, Miguel."

Miguel paused for a long time in the silent studio. Finally, he said, "This I cannot do, Joseph. You must find that answer inside of yourself, but I will give you an exercise that may help. However, you must agree to do the exercise exactly as I present it to you. Do you agree?"

"Of course, if it will help me to understand," Joseph said.

Miguel smiled and said, "Good. Then listen carefully. In the yard behind the studio there are three apple trees. Autumn is here and the apples have ripened and are dropping off the tree. Tomorrow you are to stay away from your work and rake all of the apples. While you rake, you must agree to think only of the word trust and what it means."

"But how will raking apples teach me to trust?" Joseph looked skeptically at Miguel.

"No questions now. You have agreed to do the exercise."

The following day, Joseph dressed in jeans and an old sweat shirt and collected gloves, a garden rake and a small bushel basket to collect the apples in. He began raking early in the day.

It was a fine day. There was a faint trace of fall in the air, and the sun was warm and sensuous on his back and arms. The apples rolled easily before the iron prongs of the rake and each time the rake punctured an overripe apple, the sweet smell of fermenting apples rose up from the ground

All day his small basket filled and emptied, filled and emptied collecting curly slivers of grass and crispy twigs as well as apples. Joseph perspired slightly and he felt the breeze dry the moisture and carry it down wind blending the moisture of his body with the natural moistures of the earth.

He cleared away all of the apples even climbing each tree to shake it vigorously, coaxing the loose apples to let go of their limbs. At last the yard was cleared of the rotting apples. Joseph's muscles quivered with fatigue and at last he went into his room and filled the tub with steaming water. He soaked the strain and exhaustion from his body before joining Miguel for supper. He was weary but calm.

At supper, Miguel looked at Joseph and smiled. "Well? And did you complete the task as directed?"

Joseph squirmed slightly beneath Miguel's direct gaze. He finally said, "Well, I tried to do just as you instructed, but I am afraid I did not do well at all. I would concentrate on the word trust for a moment—and then I would think only of the apples again, forgetting all about thinking of trust. I could hold my thoughts only for a brief moment during the day. I am sorry. I was just too busy to think about trust."

Miguel nodded his head and grinned. "Excellent, Joseph. Today you learned to trust."

Working with the unconscious mind can often be like chasing butterflies. The messages may be elusive, obscure, and sometimes coded. These are just a few techniques for chasing the butterflies. You have probably noticed much overlap in the techniques and you may begin to develop your own special ways of getting information from the unconscious mind. The key is that you take the time to begin developing this relationship. It will be the most important friend you have, and it will never leave you.

Daily Clearing
Once you have gone in and reframed many of the major

130

patterns, you will be able to move to a daily maintenance program. Every day you will be offered continuous opportunities to refine and strengthen the partnership with the various parts of you. If you lose track of the daily maintenance, you will again begin to experience discomfort increasing and dis-ease intensifying.

Like eating habits, you can blow your daily routine occasionally, but if blowing it becomes the new routine, you will eventually gain weight. Same thing happens here. Hatred is merely a growing collection of tiny resentments. Depression is a growing collection of self-refusals. So often the problem is not the feeling but how you feel about the feeling that leads you into darkness and chaos. Have you heard that before?

At first I found it very difficult to act in my own behalf. I slid easily back into people pleasing and being what others expected me to be. I soon discovered that that is much more painful than the risk of saying what I need to say.

The human brain is an amazing tool, but if we do not learn to use it, it will use us. It learns very quickly. Most of our moments of learning or illumination have happened in just seconds. I call those "ah ha" experiences. The beauty of the "ah ha" experience is that it happens quickly and the learning lasts a lifetime. Wouldn't it be great to begin to have control over the "ah ha" learning experience? By using these techniques, we are going for the voluntary "ah ha". Try them all and you will discover which ones fit best for you.

The techniques I have outlined work, but they also take work. I can think of no better way to begin than to buy a notebook and start a journal. Remember that a journal is a tool for change and not just a bitch book. Use these techniques or find others but use the pen and pad to open up the part of the brain that can give you the gift of self-discovery. There is no substitute for self-awareness. Emerson, in his *Essay on Self Reliance* said,

> A man should learn to detect and watch that gleam of light which flashes across his mind from within more than the luster of bards and sages. Yet he dismisses his thought, because it is his. In every work of genius we recognize our own rejected thoughts: they come back to us with a certain alienated majesty.

131

Conclusion

A Commitment to Excellence

The world is not such a happy place these days. It is out of touch with the depth and beauty of inner human awareness. Everyone is running around frantically trying to find out what they need, seeking answers in books and courses and addictions. The search for excellence is a popular topic these days but there is a missing piece in many of them—the need to look first inside of ourselves.

Trust yourself. Trust your dreams. Trust your un-conscious mind and the signals that come from a greater source of power and majesty. When you have learned to trust . . . teach others to trust as well. Teach them to be gentle and forgiving with themselves and others. Help them to understand the meaning of pain and suffering so that they can begin to satisfy the truer intentions of pain—the discovery of their own needs and a partnership with the unconscious, deeper self.

Being uncomfortable is a signal that we are missing a vital piece of the puzzle. Being happy and having a positive mental attitude does not mean never being uncomfortable. Anxiety pushes and prods us to change. And we accept the challenge because it is worth it.

Suggested Reading List

Since I first wrote this book, my own interests and many of the books mentioned have come and gone, so I would just like to include a few of what I consider my own essential reads. There are plenty of NLP books out there, and I encourage you to look into this valuable technology—it has informed every part of my life. Also, please visit my website and blog for further exploration. The addresses are listed below.

Bandler, Richard, *Using Your Brain . . . For a Change*

Fritz, Robert, *The Path of Least Resistance*

LeShan, Lawrence, *Cancer as a Turning Point*

LeShan, Lawrence, *The Psychology of War*

Pearce, Joseph Chilton, *The Magical Child Matures*

Pearce, Joseph Chilton, *Evolution's End*

Ratey, John, *User's Guide to the Brain*

Smilkstein, Rita, *We're Born to Learn*

About the Author

Patricia "Jamie" Lee, MA

Jamie Lee is a woman of great vision. Her wish is that all would live in peace exploring our lives as conscious human beings. Jamie has taught thousands of individuals to view their lives in a new way with NLP, Family Constellation Work, coaching, and other modalities.

Jamie is the author of multiple books, short stories, and nonfiction works. Her themes always include engaging life in fresh new ways. Her first novel, *Washaka* was awarded The Ben Franklin Award for Best New Voice in Fiction and was also a finalist in the PEN USA for Children's Literature.

In 2009, Jamie and her husband, Milt Lee, bought ten acres of land in northern Minnesota and began building a straw bale house. She and Milt have produced over 80 documentaries for public radio and television including the award-winning series, *Oyate Ta Olowan—The Songs of the People.* You may wish to visit their websites to learn more about their various creative works.

No Ordinary Life (Jamie's blog) at www.jamieleeonline.com

The Bead People International Peace Project at
www.thebeadpeople.org

Video Letters from Prison (a film documentary about
fathers) at www.videolettersfromprison

The Oyate Series and other documentaries at
www.oyate.com

9585408R0008

Made in the USA
Charleston, SC
24 September 2011